THE MACHINE KNITTER'S GUIDE TO THE RIBBER

BETTY BAILEY

Photography by
Ken Hoskin, AIBPP, ARPS, FMPA
and
G.A. Austin, AMPA, LIBPP

BLANDFORD PRESS
LONDON · SYDNEY · NEW YORK

First published in the UK 1988 by Blandford Press
Artillery House, Artillery Row, London SW1P 1RT

Distributed in the United States by
Sterling Publishing Co, Inc,
2 Park Avenue, New York, NY 10016

Distributed in Australia by
Capricorn Link (Australia) Pty Ltd
PO Box 665, Lane Cove, NSW 2066

British Library Cataloguing in Publication Data

Bailey, Betty
    The machine knitter's guide to the ribber.
    1. Knitting, Machine
    I. Title II. Hoskin, Ken III. Austin,
    G.A.
    746.43'2   TT680

ISBN 0 7137 1958 3

Created and written with an Amstrad PCW8256
with Amsoft Locoscript programs.

Typeset by Best-set Typesetter Ltd, Hong Kong.

Printed and bound by
Adlard and Son Limited,
Dorking, Surrey, and Letchworth, Hertfordshire

CONTENTS

ACKNOWLEDGEMENTS

The author is grateful to: Carol Williams and Pat Coulston of Metropolitan Sewing Machines for her introduction to machine knitting; Sandra Williams of Sandra Williams Publications Ltd for her introduction to writing for machine knitters; the Principal of Christchurch Adult Education Centre, Christchurch, Dorset, for the opportunity to teach machine knitters at the centre for a period of five years; all knitters who have shared their problems with her, so inspiring the writing of this book; the models and the photographers, especially Ken Hoskin for his great patience and skill in producing the majority of the photographs; and, finally, all others concerned with the production of this book, which is dedicated to machine knitters – worldwide.

AUTHOR'S NOTE

The patterns in this book, all in a wide range of sizes, are designed for the family. For that reason they have been modelled in the colour section by members of families. They are all knitting friends of the author and their friends and families, and the author is grateful for their help.

Dimensions throughout the book, including those on the diagrams, are in centimetres.

All page references in bold refer to the colour section.

A MATTER OF INTRODUCTIONS

This chapter is all about introductions. Firstly, particularly for those of you who have only just acquired a ribber, you must be introduced to it, learn how to set it up, and what it can and cannot do.

We will come back to that in a moment.

Hopefully, by the end of the course, you will realise that your ribber is an essential part of your knitting life – something from which you could not bear to be parted!

Secondly, you need to be introduced to THE COURSE (and the author).

Excuse the capitals, but for the last six or so months THE COURSE has been the centre-point of thought for me, the author. Now that it is finished, and checked – and re-checked – I can relax and write the first chapter with these very necessary introductions, and the last chapter which will view this course in retrospect.

The hope is that everyone who buys this book will also use it. If you read and knit through the eleven working chapters (2 to 12), then, when you arrive at Chapter 13 and look back over what you have achieved, you will realise just how much you have learnt.

In each chapter you will learn certain techniques, quite often knitting practice pieces which you can keep for reference. Then you will find a knitting project in which you will use the techniques you have just learnt. The patterns have been written in a wide range of sizes, so if you wish to have a permanent record of your course work, you could knit the smallest sizes.

I hope that you will not give away any of your course work until you have completed all of it. Then, in Chapter 13, you can hold a mini-exhibition, as I have done for the photography.

That deals with the course. We will come back to the author at the end of the chapter.

INTRODUCING THE RIBBER

Strictly, we should say 'Introducing the Ribbing Attachment'. That is because, in all the Japanese domestic knitting machines, the 'ribber' is a separate attachment for the main bed and cannot be used alone as the main bed can. Doubtless many readers started their knitting with a single bed (main bed) machine.

If your ribber is not already attached, let us now unpack it and do that.

Basically, putting up one make of ribber is the same as putting up any other. Part names vary slightly, and so do instruction books! Follow through the process of attaching the rib bed to the main bed from your own instruction book, working in this order.

1. Prepare the main bed. Take off the yarn mast, close the tool box, remove the carriage and any loose equipment. Remove the clamps and replace them with the large clamps from the ribber box. These lift the main bed into the tilted position which is needed when the rib bed is added.

2. Now read what your book says about attaching the rib bed to the main bed. There are fixing screws to be put into place. The three makes are all slightly different, but the functions are the same – to hold the rib bed in place, and to position it the correct distance from the main bed. Following the instructions, get the ribber out of its box and set it up...

Resolve not to take it down again except for cleaning!

3. When the two beds are connected, and the brackets at the back of the ribber are resting on the table or stand, put back the two small clamps. Their function now is to fix those brackets. They should be hand-tight, not levered tight using a tool.

4. Sit down at the machine, and, again referring to the book, get used to raising and lowering the rib bed. There are three positions in all the machines:

   a) *Knitting position* – sufficient gap to take the casting on comb and to allow both carriages to knit. This gap is very carefully controlled in modern ribbers. In older models it often required adjusting. Just make sure you understand from your book which parts of the two beds must touch.

   b) *Lower position 1* – about 2.5 cm (an inch) below knitting position. This is low enough to pick up the odd dropped stitch without all the rest of the ribber stitches sliding off the needles.

Be careful when you lower the bed one place that it does not go right down to the next position. If it does, start again − it is quicker than all that picking up. Your knee up under the centre of the bed is a good idea until you get the feel of the operation.

   c) *Lower position 2* − about 5 cm (two inches) down. This is the position for most of your single bed knitting when the ribber is attached. There is a way of knitting on the main bed with the ribber up, but that will come later. For now we are thinking about what happens when you separate the two carriages and put on the single bed sinker plate.

Do cover the rib bed − its gate pegs ruin cuffs. Some makes have special plastic covers, but they are not interchangeable between the machines. A piece of thick plastic sheeting folded over the bed and clipped together at the bottom with clothes pegs works quite well in the absence of the real thing.

5. Lower the bed (either position) and slide the ribber carriage onto it. Notice the stop knobs which prevent it falling off when the bed is lowered.

Be careful! In some cases they only prevent it crashing down provided it is pushed right back on the runners. I take mine off when it is not in use. It is easier to cover the rib bed without it, too.

Raise the bed and link the two carriages together. Make sure all the needles are in non-working position, and run the carriages backwards and forwards once or twice.

Be seated comfortably. The right height is important. Knee-room and leg-stretching room is important − if you cannot stretch your legs out you will get cramp and backache. The position you are in now is different from the one you have been used to, but if you get it right now you will be happy to keep your ribber in position. If you are tempted to take it off for single bed work, then your seating needs adjusting. You should be able to put a hand (or both hands) on the SIDE, not TOP, of the carriage handle and knit all day.

There is a tilt-stand available for Toyota and Knitmaster machines. This enables the knitter to lower the ribber and put the main bed back into the horizontal position for single bed work.

WHAT THE RIBBER CAN DO AND HOW IT WORKS
Unless you are a complete beginner to knitting, try out this experiment on the

rib bed only. If you are a beginner to machine knitting do exactly the same on the main bed, checking which controls to use from your instruction book. When you use the main bed take off the ribber arm, then you can see the needles working.

First lower the rib bed to the lowest position. Take a good look at the carriage. Compare it with the photograph, and look at the photographs of the other makes. You will notice that they all have at least five controls: two at the sides, and three others. These are the ones marked on the photographs A and B, C and D, E.

Jones + Brother KR-830 ribbing attachment

Knitmaster SRP 50 ribbing attachment

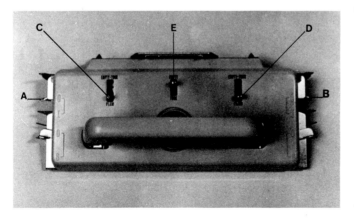

Toyota KR 501 ribbing attachment

The three types of machine have different labelling on these controls, and different names, so please check with your book, so you know the names relevant to your machine. Each letter controls the same knitting function on all of them except that the operation of E is slightly different in Toyota machines.

There are some extra controls on two of the machines, as follows:

Jones + Brother At the bottom of the rib carriage is a lever which moves between two marked positions: I and II. This is the slide lever. When in position II the rib bed needles are raised to a higher position as they knit. This means that the yarn between the stitches of the two beds is shorter, and the knitting therefore firmer and tighter. The first row of rib casting on can be knitted with the lever in position II, resulting in a much better edge. There are other occasions when this extra facility is used, but they will be described in a later book, as will the additions on the KR-850 and the Knitmaster SRP 60 ribbers.

Toyota Below the levers A and B are two similar ones, upper position marked O, and lower position marked S. These must always be set to O unless you are using the Simulknit facility in which double bed Fair Isle is knitted.

As on the main bed, there are four positions for the needles on the rib bed. These are lettered on the machine; different makes have some different letters, so for reference they are numbered here, and throughout the book will be referred to by full name or initials. They are:

1. Non-working position (NWP)	Main bed (MB)	Needles right back
	Rib bed (RB)	Needles right down
2. Working position (WP)	Both beds	Needle tips level with edge of needle bed
3. Upper working position (UWP)	Both beds	Needle tips about half an inch outside edge of needle bed
4. Holding position (HP)	Both beds	Needles pushed out or up as far as possible

The five controls on the ribber carriage, and those which are similar on the main carriage, affect the knitting according to the position of the needles. It is important to learn what each control does.

NON-WORKING POSITION
No matter how you set the carriage controls you will not knit needles which are not in work.

HOLDING POSITION

When the machine is correctly set needles in holding position will not knit; the carriage just glides over them. Put about 40 rib bed needles into working position. Set controls as shown and move the carriage across and back.

All machines A and B pushed down

No needles moved. This means they would not have knitted in either direction. LEVER A affects the needles as the carriage moves to the left, and LEVER B as it moves to the right.

Now push the levers up and move the carriage across. All the needles have moved back to working position. If there had been knitting in progress a row would have been knitted. That is an easy method of getting the knitting started again when some or all of the stitches have been in holding position. This method can always be used on the ribber, but only on the main bed provided the punchcard or electronic patterning is not being used. If pattern knitting is in progress the needles must be returned to working position by the use of a transfer tool otherwise the pattern will be interrupted by one plain row.

Find out what happens in the following cases:

Needles	Working position	Levers A and B Down
	Upper working position	Levers A and B Down

That experiment shows you that levers A and B when down only affect needles in holding position.

Now push 40 needles to holding position again, put the side levers *down* and move the carriage across. The needles are still in holding position, as you would expect. Push half the needles down to upper working position, leaving the rest in holding position and the levers down. Move the carriage over again. That is the quick way to knit the needles back into work when they have been in holding position but on the main bed it is restricted to plain knitting. The slow way is to take each stitch back to working position using a transfer tool. This is the method used on the main bed when pattern knitting.

Except when the HOLDING CAMS are being used they should be left in the upper position. This is important, because sometimes it is helpful to put end needles to holding position to help them to knit back correctly. They will only do this if the holding cams (A and B) are in the upper position.

KNITTING

Put the needles to working position and set the carriage as follows:

Jones + Brother   C and D down
Knitmaster   C and D down
Toyota   C and D down E up

Move the carriage across the needles and back. The needles move up, almost to holding position, and back to working position in a lovely wave movement. This is what happens when they knit. The yarn is placed in the hook of each needle, and, as the needle moves out the stitch already on it slips behind the latch. As the needle moves in towards working position again the stitch drops off over the closed latch. A new stitch is made from the yarn in the hook and another row has been knitted.

SLIP STITCH

Set controls C and D like this:

Jones + Brother   C and D up E down
Knitmaster   C and D up E pushed to the right
Toyota   C D E up

Move the carriage across the needles and back. This time watch the needles just 'wiggle' slightly. This is the SKIP or PART, SLIP, or EMPTY position. These are different names for the same stitch, given in order of machine as above.

Find out what happens when you have C up and D down, leaving E in position. Then reverse C and D and see what happens.

You now know how to slip (this is the most commonly used of these terms) both ways or either way. C is for slipping to the left and D to the right, never forgetting that E must also be in its proper place.

Slip stitch on the main bed is used as a pattern stitch, and there is a limited and advanced use of it for patterning on the rib bed of the Jones + Brother 850 and Knitmaster SRP 60 ribbers. One of the uses of this facility on the ribber is for moving (slipping) the carriage across to the other side without the stitches knitting. The same thing can be done on the main bed.

It does save taking the carriage off and walking round with it!

TUCK STITCH

In TUCK needles move to upper working position and back – far enough for the yarn to be collected by the hooks of the needles, but not far enough for the stitches of the previous row knitted to drop behind the latches, and off over the new yarn so knitting another row. That happens when you knit a row, but not when you tuck.

Set controls like this and knit over and back and watch the needles.

Jones + Brother   C D E up
Knitmaster   C D up E to ⌒
Toyota   C D up E down
NOTE ⌒ and ⌂ are symbols for TUCK in machine knitting books.

To tuck in one direction only:

All Machines: Leave E in tuck position
                C up D down machine tucks when knitting to left
                D up C down machine tucks when knitting to right

On the rib bed there is, at present, no pattern selecting mechanism such as is available on the main bed in punchcard or electronic selection. Doubtless it will come in time. For the moment, so far as knit, slip and tuck are concerned all the working needles act in the same way according to the cam setting.

In your ribber box there is a large knob on a metal spindle. It is the racking handle. Following the instructions, push it into place. It goes in with a click. Turn it to 5. At the left of the machine is a slide lever with left and right position. That is the pitch lever. Both these controls are used to move the rib bed sideways. Experiment with them, and watch what happens to the position of the needles of the two beds in relation to each other. Do not move the carriages, just the rib bed.

Do this with the needles in WORKING POSITION then they will not collide.

To thread your ribber (using 4 ply acrylic), push up the bed and connect the carriages. Look at your book; it shows you where the yarn should go. Make sure it does not catch on the gate pegs. It must run through freely.

YARNS AND TENSIONS

In most of the patterns a good quality 4 ply acrylic yarn has been used to knit the garments. There are four exceptions: in Chapters 7 and 10 the pattern suggests 2 ply yarn for preference, or, if not available, 2 ends (strands) of 2/30s industrial acrylic yarn. For the suit in Chapters 11 and 12 knitters are advised to use 4 ply wool, which, being heavier, hangs better.

Tension dial settings are the ones used by the author. It may be necessary to vary them slightly to obtain the same tension swatch measurements. This is because of variations in the machines, and also in different makes of yarn.

Remember, too, that even in the same make, yarns will knit differently sometimes if they are different colours. Even in the same colour a dye number can make a difference. For these reasons it is absolutely essential to knit a tension swatch every time.

MAINTAINING YOUR RIBBER

Looking after the ribber is exactly the same as looking after your main bed machine. Briefly, remove fluff and dust every time you finish knitting; oil the rails to ensure smooth running; take off the carriage, brush, clean, and oil as instructed. Never over-oil a machine; little and often is the better way. From time to time, and the frequency depends upon use, but not less than once a year, take out all the needles, and hook out the accumulated fluff from under the needle bed. Soak the needles in white spirit, wipe them clean and wipe the ends of the stems with an oily rag before putting them back. Given this kind of care a machine will last for years.

It is important that the needles of the two beds are correctly aligned vertically. To test this, set the machine to Full Pitch. Bring about 20 main bed needles at the extreme ends of the beds to holding position. Gently push up the same number of rib bed needles. If the tips of the latter touch the stems of the main bed needles the setting is correct. If they pass to the right of the main bed needles the rib bed needs moving to the left, and *vice versa*.

To correct, if necessary, loosen very slightly the two screws at the left of the face of the rib bed, remembering to use the correct screwdriver according to the head of the screw. This releases the bed and makes it possible to move it slightly sideways. Tap the end gently with the hand until the two sets of needles just touch. Tighten the screws. For further information see bibliography.

Introductions almost over! Ready to begin! Before we do, the author, already known, happily, to many of you through magazine articles, knitting exhibitions, knitting clubs, adult education classes, university courses, and even despairing telephone calls, has a personal word for all who use this book.

I am happy to have met so many of you in the past, personally or through the printed word. I hope to meet many more . . . I must thank those who asked for this book to be written; those at whose side I have sat while they learnt their craft; and, lastly, I must thank YOU for embarking on the course . . . with, sitting by your side to help and encourage . . . me, the author — your teacher and course leader.

HAPPY KNITTING!

2

1 BY 1 RIBBING: CHILD'S PIXIE HOOD

The ribbing with which the course starts is 1 by 1, also called '1 × 1'. Purl stitches, knitted on the main bed, alternate with knit stitches, knitted on the rib bed.

The method of casting on is the one given in the machine instruction books. As you work through this chapter you will be knitting a child's pixie hood in 1 by 1 ribbing, and, as with all knitted garments, a tension swatch is needed.

CASTING ON AND KNITTING THE TENSION SWATCH

1. Check pitch and carriage setting. The rib bed must be in full pitch position and both carriages set to knit.
2. Select required needles according to the following needle diagram:

```
MB    l o l o l o l o l o l
RB    o l o l o l o l o l o
```

In all the needle diagrams   MB = main bed;   RB = rib bed
l   = needle in working position
o   = needle in non-working position
s   = seaming stitch: these are shown on needle diagrams relating to
      some of the garments. They are extra to the rib arrangement, and
      are knitted so that, when the garment has been seamed together,
      the rib formation is continuous. They are always on the main bed

To select needles, use the 1 by 1 needle pusher. On the main bed, starting with the 30th needle left of centre 0, push alternate needles to working position. Continue as far as the 31st needle right of 0. On the rib bed, starting with the 29th needle left of centre, push to working position the needles which are opposite the non-working needles on the main bed.

There are 61 needles in working position for the tension swatch, not the usual 60. This is because when the ribber is used it is normal to obey what is called the 'end needle rule'. This rule says that both the end needles shall be on the main bed and not on the rib bed. If only 60 needles were in working position then at one end the last needle would be on the ribber. As with all rules there are exceptions, but they will come later.

3. Align needles in working position by running the joined carriages across them. Stop with the carriage positioned on the right.
   NOTE : Casting on, as in single bed work, can start at either side of the needle bed. The side given is the one in the instruction books.

4. Thread main yarn into the feeder on the joined carriages and drop the end between the two beds.

5. Knit the Zig Zag Row. A zig zag row is the foundation row of all ribs. Set the tension to 0/0. Most books give a higher tension, but this is seldom necessary. Proceed as follows:

Knitmaster and Toyota	Tie yarn to clamp
Jones + Brother	Hold yarn end with left hand underneath beds
All machines	Knit 1 row

The yarn now lies in a zig zag in the hooks of all working needles

6. Insert Cast On Comb. Without this it is impossible to knit ribbing. Use the shortest possible comb to cover the needles in use. Leaving the wire in position hold the comb underneath the beds. Push the right end up between the beds to the right of the knitting, positioning the comb *centrally*. Check position by the number of needles which the comb will cover.

   Slowly pull out the wire, at the same time pushing the teeth of the comb up between the beds. Pull out only enough wire to allow the comb to be raised into position. When all the teeth are above the level of the knitting push the wire through the holes. Lower the comb so the wire rests on the zig zag row. Make sure that the end of the wire does not catch on the needle bed.

15

Check this as you knit by pulling the comb down from underneath. If it gets caught up your stitches will not knit off properly, so check every row until you are sure the comb is clear.

In Jones machines put the end of the yarn into the clip on the comb.

Comb inserted

The comb and wire have two functions. Firstly, the wire holds down the yarn of the zig zag row to allow the next row to be knitted.

If you forget to insert the comb you will have a terrible muddle!

Secondly, the comb has holes in it for hanging the weights.

In the single bed carriage the brushes help to pull the stitches over the closed latches containing the yarn from the feeder. When you are ribbing the weights carry out this function.

According to instruction books the weights should be hung before knitting any further. This is not necessary if you are using the cast on comb with the bar which is standard equipment with Jones + Brother machines. The weights can stretch the zig zag, and also break fine yarn. Hang them now or when the ribbing is started according to the type of comb you are using.

Hang two large weights underneath the knitting, not outside it. Place them evenly.

As you gain experience you will learn how many weights you need. It depends partly on the width of the work, partly on the texture of the yarn (springy yarn needs more weighting than soft yarn), and partly on the type of rib. In your instruction book there is guidance on this matter. Read it, let it guide you, but you decide!

Three points to remember. Firstly, if your ribber is set up and adjusted correctly you will not need as many weights as if it is not correctly aligned. Check the setting from time to time. Secondly, use only just enough weight to enable the ribber to knit off the stitches correctly. Thirdly, it is usually better to use two small weights rather than one weight alone when you use a cast on comb. With one weight the comb tends to tip up.

7. Knitting the Selvedge. The selvedge consists of several rows knitted first on one bed and then on the other. These are called tubular or circular rows. The carriages are set so that the beds knit and slip alternately. Always knit at least two rows for a selvedge, because they make a complete circle. Sometimes knitters prefer to knit three or four rows. It does not normally matter which bed slips first, so follow what your instruction book says. Set the carriages so that the main bed knits the first and third rows, the rib bed the second. If you cannot remember carriage settings, go back to Chapter 1.

   With tension still 0/0 knit 3 rows, stopping at the end of each to see how circular rows are formed. The carriage will be at the right, which is where many pattern instructions, including those in this book, start. It is therefore convenient to finish welts at that side. If you wish to knit 2 or 4 rows of selvedge, knit 1 extra row of rib to finish welts on the right.

Three selvedge rows

8. Knit 1 × 1 ribbing. Tension 3/3. Set both carriages to knit in both directions. (Refer to Chapter 1.)

   Hang two large weights underneath the knitting, not outside it. Place them evenly. Knit 1 row. Examine the stitch formation of the first row of rib.

Knit 6 rows of rib altogether.

Break off main yarn leaving about a foot (30 cm) above the feed. Tie the end of the waste yarn to this. Pull it down throgh the yarn feed until it is correctly threaded. Secure the end. Knit 4 rows.

This is a quick and safe way of feeding in another colour when you do not have a colour changer in use. It is all too easy to take out one yarn, and thread in another carelessly, knit a row, and down it all falls. Do check threading.

Change back to main yarn. Set row counter to 000. Knit 30 rows.

Take two pieces of waste yarn about 20 cm (8 inches) long. Use them to mark the 21st stitch either side of 0. On the left this will be on the rib bed, on the right on the main bed. First knit the stitch manually on to the waste yarn, then thread both ends into the transfer needle and drop them between the beds.

Knit 30 more rows. RC 60 (sometimes shown as RC 060).

Change to waste yarn. Knit 6 rows. Normally the yarn would be broken off and the work released from the machine.

We will use the sample to practise transferring rib bed stitches to the main bed using the transfer needle.

First use the needle pusher to push all rib bed needles up so that the stitches are just behind the latches.

Keeping transfer tool in a straight line with first rib bed needle, put eye of tool over hook of needle. Push gently down until the stitch slides over closing latch onto transfer tool.

Rib bed needles pushed up so stitches are behind latches

First stitch halfway there

This stitch is nearly there. Be careful not to drop it! If you do, don't panic! When, not 'if', you drop a stitch (it happens to everyone) follow this procedure:

a) Take off weights – that stops the dropped stitch running further.

b) Lower the rib bed one position – carefully, and one position only. If dropped stitch is near an end, lower that end only.

c) Pick up stitch and, if it is a main bed stitch, return it to its needle knitting it up manually a row at a time. If it is a rib bed stitch, use the latch tool to knit it up, taking care not to miss any 'ladder rungs'.

d) Put on the weights to stop any more stitches jumping off as you raise the bed and carry on with the work.

19

Slide the stitch along the transfer tool and off the other end into the hook of the main bed needle opposite.

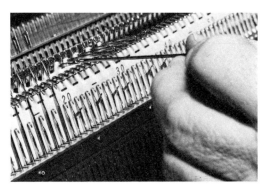

First stitch transferred

Repeat until all stitches are on the main bed.

Change to waste yarn. Leave ribber raised, rib carriage attached and weights in position. Knit 6 rows. Remove weights. Release from machine.

Notice how you can use the main bed only without changing to the single bed sinker plate: ribber up; ribber carriage connected; weights on.

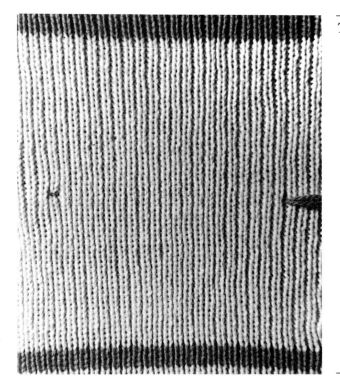

Tension swatch 1 × 1 rib

9. Blocking Out and Measuring Acrylic Yarn Tension Swatch. Place knitting on flat surface and leave to relax overnight. Pin out swatch on blocking board stretching the width slightly. Press very lightly under dry cloth. Leave to cool. Remove pins. Measure 40 stitches and 60 rows.

The measurements of the swatch used for garment shown on Page 1 were:

36 stitches and 44 rows = 10 cm (4 inches)

TO KNIT THE PIXIE HOOD

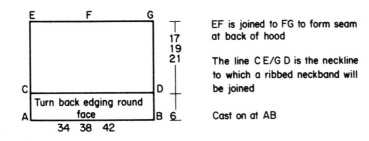

EF is joined to FG to form seam at back of hood

The line C E/G D is the neckline to which a ribbed neckband will be joined

Cast on at AB

	S	M	L
Sizes: Small, Medium, Large Check size from measurements on garment block.			

Main Piece

	S	M	L
Arrange needles of both beds for 1 × 1 rib as follows	123	137	151
Edging Using contrast yarn cast on and knit selvedge. RC 000. Tension 3../3... Knit to RC	26	28	30
Main Part Change to main colour. RC 000. Tension 3/3. Knit to RC. Cast off in rib. Tension 6/6.	74	84	92

All Sizes Knit 1 row. Transfer all stitches to main bed. Push all needles to holding position so that stitches do not spring off needles when comb and weights are removed. After removing them cast off using latch tool.

Neckband

	S	M	L
Arrange needles of both beds for 1 × 1 rib as follows	123	137	151
Using main yarn cast on and knit selvedge. RC 000. Tension 3/3. Knit to RC. Cast off in rib. Tension 6/6.	18	20	22

All Sizes Knit 1 row.
This time try another method of casting off. Do not transfer stitches to main bed. Remove comb and weights. Hang some claw weights. Cast off using latch tool working across the beds from main bed stitch to rib bed stitch right along the row.

To Make Up Fold main piece of hood together at cast off edge. Seam neatly on inside, or crochet together through cast off chain stitches on outside. Place cast off edge of neckband to neck edge of hood. Oversew together on wrong side. Make two button loops on right of neckband, Sew buttons on left side.

NOTE: Ties of any description at the neck of a garment are *dangerous* to children and should *never* be used. Fold edging back and sew ends to top of neckband.

TO RECAP

In this chapter you have learnt:
- *how to cast on and knit 1 by 1 rib*
- *how to weight the work*
- *how to make a tension swatch in rib*
- *how to transfer stitches to the main bed*
- *how to cast off in rib by two methods...and...very important...*
- *how to pick up dropped stitches!*

3

FISHERMAN'S RIB: SIMPLE OVERTOP

Fisherman's rib is an automatic tuck stitch pattern. It is knitted using the 1 by 1 rib needle setting, tucking on the main bed when knitting in one direction, and on the rib bed when knitting in the other. It does not matter which bed tucks in which direction.

In Chapter 1 we found out how to set the rib carriage for tuck, and you revised the settings of the main carriage if you needed to. When you come to set your machine, if you cannot remember how to set the controls go back and check before you start knitting.

CASTING ON AND KNITTING THE TENSION SWATCH
All stages of casting on for any rib follow the same pattern.

Look back to Chapter 2 if you cannot remember how to carry out any part. The numbers of each step are the same as in the previous chapter. You will not always need to look back — casting on will soon be something you do automatically.

1. Rib bed in full pitch position.
2. Select needles for 1 by 1 rib.
3. Align needles.
4. Thread main yarn into carriage feeder.
5. Zig zag row. Tension 0/0.
6. Insert comb.
7. Selvedge. Tension 1/1. Knit 3 rows.
    Selvedge tension is higher than for 1 by 1 rib because this is a tuck rib, and therefore, like all tuck stitches, wide. Too tight a tension would tighten the beginning of the knitting.
8a. Set carriages for Fisherman's rib so that main bed tucks to the left, rib bed tucks to the right. Tension 4/4. Knit 1 row.

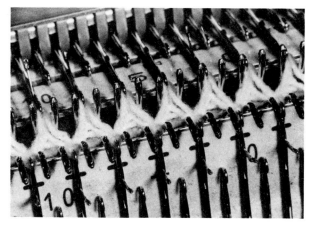

First row: Main bed tucks, rib bed knits

Knit another row.

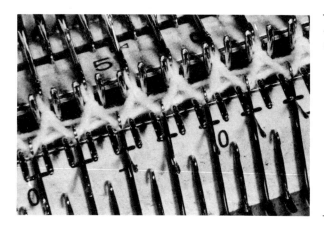

Second row: Main bed knits, rib bed tucks

Knit 8 rows. Change to contrast yarn. Knit 4 rows.
Change to main yarn. RC 000. Knit 30 rows.
Mark 21st stitch either side of 0. Knit 30 rows.
Change to waste yarn. Knit 8 rows.

The tension swatch is finished, but we will use it to practise increasing and decreasing.

8b. Increasing by the end stitch method. This means bringing an extra needle into working position at the carriage end.

The end needle is a main bed one, so the first increase will be on the rib bed. The second increase will be on the main bed. RC 000.

Increase as follows:

Row 1   Bring 1 extra needle to working position on rib bed at right.

Knit 1 row. An extra stitch has been formed at right.
Row 2 Bring 1 extra needle to working position on rib bed at left.
Knit 1 row. An extra stitch has been formed at left.
Rows 3, 4 Knit without increasing.
Rows 5–8 Repeat rows 1–4 increasing on the main bed.

Knit to RC 40 noting that alternate increasings are on opposite beds. As the knitting becomes wider there is less tension on the new stitches than there is on the original ones. Put the side weight hangers in position between the beds at the ends of the work and hang small weights on them.

Putting in a wire hanger for a side weight

In a pattern the increasing instructions would probably read:

Increase 1 stitch at both ends of the next row and every following 4th row 10 times.

It is easier to increase 1 stitch at the beginning of each of the first 2 rows as in the instructions you have just followed. The pattern instructions in this chapter make this clear.

You have just broken the End Needle Rule – several times...
No problems, were there?

8c. Casting off in rib. *Cancel tuck setting.* Tension 8/8. Knit 1 row.

Again a higher tension because of the width of the fabric.

Cast off using one of the methods learnt in the last chapter.
9. Block out and rest fabric. Measure 40 stitches and 60 rows.

25

Sample of Fisherman's rib. Notice the shadowy depths of the purl side showing the columns of knit stitches

The measurements of the swatch used for garment shown on Page 1 were:

25 stitches and 66 rows = 10 cm (4 inches)

These are the measurements which will be used in the pattern. They are also the ones required for Knitmaster Radar. The 'green ruler' method used for finding out, from 40 stitches and 60 rows marked in the normal way on any tension swatch, how many stitches and rows are needed to knit 10 cm, is the easiest way to obtain these measurements from the tension swatch. (Knitters who do not have a green ruler with their machine can obtain one, together with full instructions for its use, from most knitting machine stockists.)

FISHERMAN'S RIB COMPARED WITH 1 BY 1 RIBBING

Two differences between the two tension swatches are immediately obvious. Fisherman's rib is thicker than 1 by 1 rib because of the tucking, and the piece of fabric is both wider and shorter than the first sample.

It is easier to compare the measurements if we measure in centimetres the width of 40 stitches and the depth of 60 rows. These are the measurements needed for the Jones + Brother Knitleader and the Toyota Knitracer. They are as follows:

| 40 stitches: | 1 × 1 rib: 11 cm | Fisherman's rib: | 16 cm |
| 60 rows: | 13.5 cm | | 9 cm |

We need fewer stitches but more rows in Fisherman's rib.

26

TO KNIT THE OVERTOP

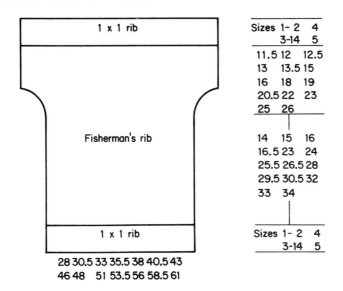

1 x 1 rib	Sizes 1- 2 4
	3-14 5
	11.5 12 12.5
	13 13.5 15
	16 18 19
	20.5 22 23
	25 26
Fisherman's rib	14 15 16
	16.5 23 24
	25.5 26.5 28
	29.5 30.5 32
	33 34
1 x 1 rib	Sizes 1- 2 4
	3-14 5

28 30.5 33 35.5 38 40.5 43
46 48 51 53.5 56 58.5 61

Long Pieces of Ribbing – Re-hanging the Comb

From the block of the overtop you will see that it is knitted entirely in ribbing. The total length of the largest size is 70 centimetres. Long before several of the larger sizes are completed the weights will be down to the floor. This is because, as you will have discovered already, the knitting stretches quite a lot as you work, and only relaxes back to its proper length some time after it is removed from the machine.

If the weights do touch the floor all the tension will go from the knitting, and the stitches will not knit off properly. Watch the work carefully as it grows longer, and before that happens, re-hang the comb in one of the following ways, depending on the kind of comb in use.

First, the special ribber comb with a bar which is part of the standard ribber equipment for Jones + Brother machines. This can also be purchased separately for use with other machines, and is now available from Knitmaster too. It is a valuable accessory as it can be used to re-hang even the widest piece of knitting. Remove the weights. Next release the knitting from the comb by pulling out the wire. Push the wire back into place. Hold the knitting on your lap, and pull it through the space between the teeth and the bar, with the teeth against the wrong side if there is any difference. Turn the comb over so that the knitting is sandwiched between the teeth and the bar. Still holding your work, place two weights evenly in the holes. Gently hang the work, taking care not to unbalance it or the comb will slide sideways. Refer to the instruction book.

If you are using an ordinary comb, hang several claw weights on the knitting before removing it. Push the teeth of the released comb through between the beds, taking care not to dislodge any stitches. Replace the wire and re-hang the weights.

To Fit Bust Sizes Centimetres	56	61	66	71	76	81	86	91	96	102	107	112	117	122
Inches	22	24	26	28	30	32	34	36	38	40	42	44	46	48

Check size from measurements on garment block.

Knit Back and Front Alike

Arrange needles for 1 × 1 rib as follows	69	75	81	87	95	101	107	115	119	127	133	139	145	153

Welt Using main yarn cast on and knit selvedge. RC 000. Tension 3/3. Knit to RC   18   18   All other sizes 22

Main Part Set machine for Fisherman's rib. RC 000. Tension 4/4. Knit to RC	92	100	106	108	152	158	168	174	184	194	202	210	218	224

Increasing at Armhole RC 000.
Increase 1 stitch at beginning of next 2 rows. Knit 2 more rows.

Repeat from * to * times in all.	8	8	8	8	8	10	10	12	12	12	12	14	14	14
Number of stitches	85	91	97	103	111	121	127	139	143	151	157	167	173	181
RC	32	32	32	32	32	40	40	48	48	48	48	56	56	56
Knit to RC	76	80	82	86	90	100	106	118	126	134	144	152	164	172

Neck and Shoulder Rib Set machine for 1 × 1 rib. RC 000. Tension 3/3. Knit to RC   18   18 All other sizes 22
Tension 8/8. Knit 1 row. Cast off using latch tool and preferred method.

Arm Bands Before knitting arm bands seam shoulders together matching ribs. Leave part of either or both shoulders of first four sizes open for button and loop fastenings.

Arrange needles for 1 × 1 rib as follows:	77	83	89	93	97	101	107	113	121	129	139	139	153	161

Cast on and knit selvedge. RC 000.
Tension 3/3. Knit to RC   18   18 All other sizes 22
Transfer all stitches to main bed. With wrong side of garment facing place side loops of armhole on same needles.

Attaching garment to armband

Tension 10. Knit 1 row. Remove comb and weights. Cast off with latch tool.

To Make Up   Sew up side seams and fasten off all ends. Fasten shoulder(s) of first four sizes with buttons and loops.

TO RECAP
In this chapter you have learnt:
>*how to cast on and knit Fisherman's rib*
>*how to increase 1 stitch at the beginnings of rows*
>*how to use side weights*
>*how to join a ribbed arm band to a garment on the machine...and...*
>*how the End Needle Rule can sometimes be broken!*

4

ENGLISH RIB: PAIR OF LEGWARMERS

English rib is another rib using tuck stitch. It is also known as Half-fisherman's or Single Fisherman's rib, because the tucking is only done on one bed, and in one direction, while the other bed knits all the time. It does not matter which bed is set to tuck, but it does make a difference to which side of the knitting is the right side, as we shall see in an experiment with the tension swatch. Another name for this stitch is Brioche stitch, after the little fat French rolls. You can see why if you look at the photograph.

Sample of English rib

CASTING ON AND KNITTING TENSION SWATCH
The first seven stages are exactly the same as for Fisherman's rib in Chapter 3.

1. Rib bed in full pitch position.
2. Select needles for 1 × 1 rib.
3. Align needles.
4. Thread main yarn into feeder.

5. Zig zag row. Tension 0/0.
6. Insert comb.
7. Selvedge. Tension 1/1. Knit 3 or 4 rows according to machine used.
8a. Set main carriage to tuck to the left. Set rib carriage to knit in both directions.

Tension 4/4. Knit 20 rows stopping occasionally to become familiar with the stitch formation.

Change to contrast yarn. Change the setting of the machine so that the rib carriage tucks to the left and the main carriage knits in both directions. Knit 8 rows. Change to main yarn. RC 000.

Knit 60 rows marking the 21st stitches at RC 30. Stop and inspect the different stitch formation from the first 20 rows.

Change to waste yarn. Knit 8 rows. Now we will practise decreasing.
8b. Decreasing on the end stitches.

Both ends are decreased in the same row.

It is more convenient to decrease when there are no tuck stitches on the needles. We shall decrease when the carriage is at the right, and this will be after both beds have knitted because the machine was set to tuck to the left.

Decrease 1 stitch at both ends every 4 rows as follows:

Row 1   Transfer both end stitches on to the needles holding the end stitches on the opposite bed. Knit 1 row.
Rows 2–4   Knit 3 rows without decreasing.
Repeat Rows 1–4 10 times in all noting that decreasings, like increasings in the previous chapter, are first on the main bed then on the rib bed.

8c. Cast off in rib. Tension 8/8. Knit 1 row. Using the latch tool cast off by one of the methods used in the previous chapter.
9. Block out and rest fabric. Measure as before.

The measurements of the swatch for garment shown on Pages 1 and 5 were:

28 stitches and 56 rows = 10 cm (4 inches)

Before knitting the legwarmers examine the tension swatch. Place it with the yarn end from the casting on at the right as it was when on the machine.

In the first part when you tucked on the main bed, as far as the stripe of waste yarn, the fat stitches were facing you as you knitted.

In the rest of the swatch, when you tucked on the rib bed the fat stitches were underneath, which means they were away from you when you knitted.

The fat stitches are the right side of the fabric, and are on the opposite side to the tucking bed. Sometimes it is convenient to choose whether to have the right side or the wrong side facing you as you are knitting.

If you stretch the knitting lengthwise and look at it closely you can see a small stitch between each fat stitch. The stitches this side were the ones made by the bed which did not tuck. That bed knits twice as many rows as the one which does tuck. That is why the stitches of half the rows are fat – they are pushed out sideways in each row where the tucking bed knits off a stitch and a tuck together.

Now and again English rib goes wrong.

If you know what this looks like on the machine it saves the heart-break of finding out after you have finished the piece of knitting.

Look carefully at the photograph below.

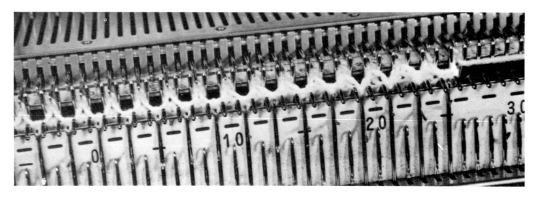

Correct knitting on the left, faulty knitting on the right

At the left the knitting is correct. You can tell this is so by the even appearance of the stitches on both beds. From stitch 17 on the rib bed to the right hand end the knitting is going wrong. The rib bed needles are higher than they should be, and the knitting is bunched up on the main bed needles. The finished knitting will not show columns of fat stitches. Instead there will be twice as many stitches at that side, and they will all be small ones because the tucking was not taking place correctly.

This fault occurs when the tuck stitches do not knit off correctly. It is sometimes caused by the tension on the edge of the work getting slack as the knitting grows longer. This can happen in all rib knitting, but especially where tuck stitches are involved. The remedy for that is to use side weights, and by keeping a watchful eye on the stitch formation as the knitting progresses, to avoid trouble.

Lack of tension is sometimes caused by yarn becoming hooked up on a main bed gate peg.

'Gate peg-itis'! You can tell when this has happened because the comb does not descend at that end. If you feel underneath (or lie on your back on the floor and look up!) you will find the offending loop. When you discover what the problem is all the needles of both beds should be put into holding position very carefully to prevent the stitches jumping off since the knitting is often very slack. Be sure that you do not unknit any as you do this. Next take the work hook and lift the loop off the gate peg. Immediately the comb will descend to a level position. Go on knitting, but NOT before you have done two things. Firstly you must put the stitches of the next bed to tuck back to working position using a transfer tool. . .IF YOU DO NOT, THEY WILL KNIT, NOT TUCK.

Secondly you should check the knitting formation right along the row correcting any 'bunching' caused by the hold-up, and re-knitting any unknitted stitches. You may even have to undo a few rows to get the work right.

This problem can also be caused if the needles of the two beds are not correctly lined up. Check the alignment regularly as suggested in Chapter 1. Make certain that yarn mast tension is correct and that no needles or latches are bent.

TO KNIT THE LEGWARMERS

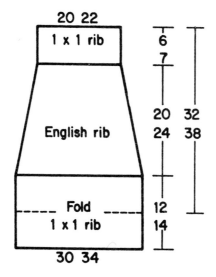

The legwarmer pattern is given in one size, the first set of measurements on the block. This is suitable for a girl of about 4 to 8 years. At the end you will find instructions for writing the pattern in the size for the other measurements. The method can be adapted for other sizes.

The legwarmers are knitted downwards from knee to ankle. You can tell this is so because on the block the wider end for the calf is at the bottom of the drawing. The direction of knitting on blocks should always be from the bottom to the top of a piece. This is the way it hangs from the machine.

Knit 2 Alike

Arrange needles of both beds for 1 × 1 rib as follows	85
Top Welt Using main yarn cast on and knit selvedge. RC 000. Tension 3/3. Knit to RC	52
Calf Section Set machine for English rib with either bed tucking to the left on the first row. RC 000. Tension 4/4. Knit to RC	8
Decrease 1 stitch at both ends of next row and every following 8th row 14 times in all. RC	112
Stitches remaining	57
Ankle Welt Set machine for 1 × 1 rib. RC 000. Tension 3/3. Knit to RC	26
Tension 8/8. Knit 1 row. Cast off in rib.	

To Make Up Mattress stitch seams carefully matching decreasings.

NOTE : If a colour changer is available the knitting can be striped. It is more effective to knit not less than 4 rows in each colour. If using a colour changer it will be necessary to start the English rib on the left of the needle bed. In this case tuck from left to right for convenience when decreasing.

REWRITING THE PATTERN IN OTHER SIZES

We will take, as an example, the second set of measurements on the block.

Top	34 cm
Ankle	22
1 × 1 top welt	14
English rib section	24
1 × 1 ankle welt	7

To work out rows or stitches: multiply the 10 cm (4 inch) row or stitch number by required length or width and divide by 10:

    1 × 1 rib   36 stitches 44 rows = 10 cm (4 inches)

    English rib   28 stitches 56 rows = 10 cm (4 inches)

All stitch and row numbers are rounded up or down as is most convenient.

Our example:

Rows:	English rib		$56 \times 24 \div 10 = 134$
	1×1 welts	Top welt	$44 \times 14 \div 10 = 60$
		Ankle welt	
		(half top welt)	30
Stitches:	English rib only	Top	$28 \times 34 \div 10 = 95$
		Ankle	$28 \times 22 \div 10 = 61$
Decrease:	At both sides		$95 - 61 \div 2 = 17$
	To calculate frequency of decreasing		
	divide rows of English rib by number of		
	decreasings:		$134 \div 17 = 7.8$

It looks from that as if we ought to decrease every 7th row. That means decreasing when the carriage is on the right and on the left alternately. (RC 7 left; 14 right; 21 left...) When it is on the left there will be tuck stitches on whichever bed is set to tuck. That means three loops on the end needle when the stitch has been decreased, which is not a good idea — too thick and clumsy. You can avoid it in two ways. Either, think ahead, before you knit the row, and make the needle knit instead of tucking by putting it to upper working position, or, if you forget to do that, latch it off by hand, that is knit it by hand, before decreasing.

The pattern would be:
1. Cast on 95 stitches.
2. 1×1 rib. Knit 60 rows.
3. Change to English rib. Knit 7 rows.
4. Decrease 1 stitch at both ends of the next row and every following 7th row, 17 times in all. RC 119.
5. Knit straight to RC 134.
6. Change to 1×1 rib. Knit 30 rows.
7. Cast off.

There is another way of arranging the decreasing. Sometimes in a pattern you will see:

Decrease (or increase) 1 stitch at both ends every 6/8 rows 17 times in all.

Occasionally it is printed out in full as 'every 6th and 8th row alternately', for that is what it means.

Decrease on the   6th row knit 8 rows = RC 14
Decrease on the 14th row knit 6 rows = RC 20
Decrease on the 20th row knit 8 rows = RC 28, and so on

A decreasing list is an essential aid to the memory:

   6 14 20 28 34 42 48 56 62 70 76 84 90 98 104 112 118

Step 4 in the pattern would then finish at row 118 – hardly any difference. Look out for decreasings written like this in some of the patterns. It is sometimes necessary to do this in order to work the number of shapings needed into the rows which are to be knitted.

TO RECAP
In this chapter you have learnt:
    how to knit English rib
    how to decrease 1 stitch at the ends of rows
    how to avoid a possible problem when knitting English rib...and...
    how to calculate a simple pattern from alternative measurements.

5

2 BY 2 RIBBING:
WELTS AND SINGLE-THICKNESS ROUND NECKBAND FOR A SINGLE BED STOCKING STITCH JUMPER

The rib known to handknitters as '2 plain 2 purl' is a very popular one because of its elastic qualities. It keeps its shape better, on the whole, than 1×1 ribbing, particularly when knitted in yarns spun from man-made fibres. In machine knitting there are two needle arrangements for 2 by 2 ribbing. The first one is dealt with in this chapter and in Chapters 6 and 8, and the second one in Chapter 7.

CASTING ON AND KNITTING TENSION SWATCH
1. Rib bed in full pitch position. Set racking handle to position 5.
2. Select needles.

```
MB    | | o o | | o o | | o o | | o o | |
RB    o o | | o o | | o o | | o o | | o o
```

3. Align needles.
4. Thread main yarn.
5. Zig zag row. Beginners only, knit 1 row.

This is what you have knitted – clearly not a zig zag row

It is impossible, in these circumstances, to hang the comb so that it holds down all the stitches. This means that the selvedge rows will not knit properly.

To knit a zig zag row the needles in work must be arranged alternately between the two beds. To do this we have to make two moves.

Firstly the pitch lever is moved to half pitch. This brings the needles to the position shown here:

```
MB    | | o o | | o o | | o o | | o o | |
RB      o o | | o o | | o o | | o o | | o
```

Did you notice that the rib bed moved to the right when the pitch lever was moved? This brought the rib bed needles halfway between the main bed needles.

The second move needed to form a zig zag is to turn the racking handle one position anti-clockwise, to 4 in Jones + Brother and Knitmaster and to 6 in Toyota. The effect on the needles is this

```
MB    | | o o | | o o | | o o | | o o | |
RB    † o o | | o o | | o o | | o o | |
```

Now there is a zig zag row except on the left. To solve that problem push a temporary extra rib bed needle into working position at '†'. Tension 0/0. Knit zig zag row.

6. Hang comb.

Zig zag row knitted

Look at the peculiar slanted zig zag. If you knit the three selvedge rows now, that unbalanced 'V' will remain for ever! That is one of the causes of dissatisfaction about 2 × 2 casting on. This, therefore, is where we depart from what we are told in the instruction books, and use a very simple method for obtaining a neater result.

7. Before knitting selvedge move back to the needle position in Paragraph 2 by racking to 5, and putting the rib bed back to full pitch. At the left on the rib bed there is still the extra needle which is not needed any more. Transfer the loop on it to the end needle on the main bed.

This is how it now appears

Selvedge. Tension 0/0. Knit 3 rows.

This method gives a much neater result. Why not try both ways so you can test it yourself? There are further improvements to be made especially when using fine yarn. We will deal with those in the next chapter.

8. Set both carriages to knit. Set tension at Stocking Stitch Tension – 2. Tension 4/4. Knit 8 rows. Change to main yarn. RC 000. Knit 60 rows. There is no need to mark 40 stitches; only the row count is needed.

   Transfer stitches to the empty needles on the main bed. Tension 6/6. Using waste yarn knit 6 rows. Release from the machine.

9. Block out and rest fabric, in doing so stretch it widthwise so that it is pinned out to appear as it will be when worn. Doing that shortens the fabric. Measure the length as before.

   Measurement of swatch used for garment shown on Pages 1 and 6 is:

   40 rows = 10 cm (4 inches)

TO KNIT THE JUMPER

First you need a stocking stitch tension swatch in the main yarn. Using Tension 6, measurements of swatch used for garment shown on Pages 1 and 6 were:

   30 stitches and 40 rows = 10 cm (4 inches)

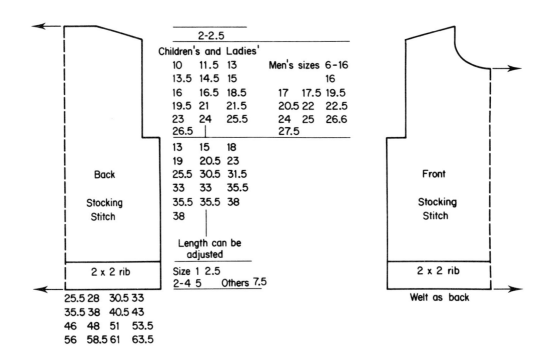

2-2.5

Children's and Ladies'

10	11.5	13	Men's sizes 6-16		
13.5	14.5	15			16
16	16.5	18.5	17	17.5	19.5
19.5	21	21.5	20.5	22	22.5
23	24	25.5	24	25	26.6
26.5			27.5		

13	15	18
19	20.5	23
25.5	30.5	31.5
33	33	35.5
35.5	35.5	38
38		

Length can be adjusted

Size 1 2.5
2-4 5   Others 7.5

Back

Stocking
Stitch

2 x 2 rib

25.5	28	30.5	33
35.5	38	40.5	43
46	48	51	53.5
56	58.5	61	63.5

Front

Stocking
Stitch

2 x 2 rib

Welt as back

19	21.5	23	24	25.5	Children's and Ladies'
28	30.5	32	34	37	
38	39.5	40.5	42	43 44.5	
31	33.5	35	37	40	Men's
41	42.5	43.5	45	46 47.5	

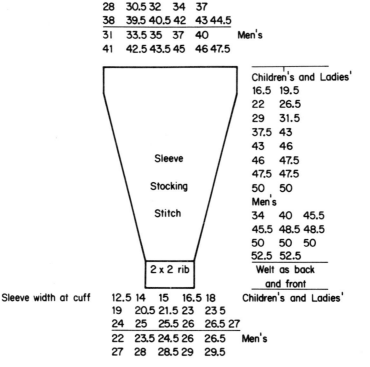

Children's and Ladies'
16.5	19.5
22	26.5
29	31.5
37.5	43
43	46
46	47.5
47.5	47.5
50	50

Men's
34	40	45.5
45.5	48.5	48.5
50	50	50
52.5	52.5	

Welt as back
and front

Sleeve

Stocking

Stitch

2 x 2 rib

Sleeve width at cuff

Children's and Ladies'
12.5	14	15	16.5	18
19	20.5	21.5	23	23 5
24	25	25.5	26	26.5 27

Men's
22	23.5	24.5	26	26.5
27	28	28.5	29	29.5

Back

To Fit Chest/Bust Sizes																
Centimetres	46	51	56	61	66	71	76	81	86	91	97	102	107	112	117	122
Inches	18	20	22	24	26	28	30	32	34	36	38	40	42	44	46	48

Back

Arrange needles for 2 × 2 rib as follows

74	82	90	98	102*	110*	118*	126*	134	142	150	158	162*	174	182	190

Welt Using main yarn cast on and knit selvedge. RC 000. Tension 4/4. Knit to RC

12 24 24   24 All other sizes 36

Main Part Transfer stitches to main bed. Increase 1 stitch both ends sizes marked * to Tension 6. RC 000. Knit to RC

74	82	90	98	104	112	120	128	134	142	150	158	164	174	182	190
52	60	72	76	82	92	102	122	126	132	132	142	142	142	152	152

NOTE : Adjust length if necessary: 10 rows = 2.5 cm = 1 inch. Sleeves on men's garments have been made wider and longer. Armhole length has been adjusted for this.

Armhole Shaping RC 000. At beginning of next 2 rows cast off

Armhole / rows																
cast off	8	9	10	11	12	12	14	16	16	17	17	18	19	20	21	22
Number of stitches remaining	58	64	70	76	80	88	92	96	102	108	116	122	126	134	140	146

Knit to RC

Children's and Ladies'	40	46	52	54	58	60	64	66	74	78	84	86	92	96	102	106
Men's						66	70	72	80	84	90	92	98	102	108	112

Shoulder Shaping by use of holding position in groups as follows at both ends, always putting the next group into holding position at the opposite end to the carriage. Wrap inside needles to prevent holes

	5	6	6	7	6	6	6	6	6	6	7	8	8	7	7	8
	5	5	6	7	5	6	6	5	6	6	7	7	8	7	7	8
	5	5	6	6	5	6	6	5	6	6	7	7	7	7	7	8
					5	5	6	5	5	6	7	7	7	7	7	7
								5	5	6	6	7	7	6	7	7
														6	7	7

Shoulder stitches	15	16	18	20	21	23	24	26	28	30	34	36	37	40	42	45
Total rows for shaping	6	6	6	6	8	8	8	10	10	10	10	10	10	12	12	12
Children's and Ladies' RC	46	52	58	60	66	68	72	76	84	88	94	96	102	108	114	118
Men's RC						74	78	82	90	94	100	102	108	114	120	124
Back neck stitches	28	32	34	36	38	42	44	44	46	48	48	50	52	54	56	56

Change to waste yarn. Knit 6 rows waste separately on stitches of both shoulders and back neck. Release all 3 sections.

Front

Knit as back to RC after Armhole

28	34	34	36	38	40	40	46	52	52	56	60	64	64	68	70

Children's and Ladies' RC

					46	46	52	56	58	62	66	70	70	74	76

Men's RC

Divide for Neck Put all stitches left of centre to holding position together with following number right of centre

8	9	10	11	11	12	12	12	12	13	13	13	14	14	14	14

Right Half Put 1 stitch at neck edge to holding position every row following number of times

6	7	7	7	8	9	10	10	11	11	11	12	12	13	14	14

Knit to RC

40	46	52	54	58	60	64	66	74	78	84	86	92	96	102	106

Children's and Ladies'

					66	70	72	80	84	90	92	98	102	108	112

Men's

Shoulder Shaping on stitches in working position at right. Shape as shoulder on back. Release shoulder stitches on waste knitting leaving neck stitches at right in holding position.

Left Half Take carriage to left. Reset row counter for start of neck shaping. Leaving centre neck stitches in holding position bring remaining stitches at left to upper working position. Shape neck and shoulder as on right. Release shoulder on waste knitting, except for small sizes, where a placket opening is necessary. Therefore, in small sizes only, knit 1 row at Tension 10 on stitches of shoulder, and cast off using latch tool. At straight edges at both sides of neck curve pick up loops and place on needles either side of curve.

Following stitches from both sides

4	4	7	7	7	7	8	8	8	9	10	10	10	12	13	14

Release holding cam. Tension

6. Knit 1 row. Change to waste yarn. Knit 6 rows.
NOTE : All stitches for back and front neckline are now held on waste yarn.

Right Shoulder Seam Before knitting neckband seam right shoulder. Replace back right shoulder stitches on needles, right side facing. Using needle pusher push needles just far enough forward to allow stitches to fall behind latches. Replace front right shoulder stitches in hooks of same needles, wrong side facing. Using needle pusher pull needles back to working position. Stitches of back bed will knit off over stitches of front bed. Tension 10. Knit 1 row. Cast off using latch tool. Before knitting neckband knit placket on back left shoulder in smallest sizes as follows:

Shoulder Placket
Wrong side of back facing pick up stitches of left shoulder. Tension 6. Knit 6 rows. Tension 8. Knit 1 row. Tension 5... Knit 6 rows. Pick up loops of first row and place on same needles. Tension 10. Knit 1 row. Cast off with latch tool.

Neckband

Arrange needles for 2 × 2 rib as follows

66 74 82 86 90 98 106 106 110 114 118 122 126 134 138 142

NOTE : Add 4 stitches for any garment with placket. Cast on and knit selvedge as before. RC 000. Knit 4 rows at each of the following tensions: 3/3 3./3. 3../3.. 4/4. RC 12. Knitting at gradually increasing tensions makes

the neckband lie flat.
Transfer to main bed. Sizes
1, 2, 7–9, 11–14, 16.
Decrease 1 stitch both ends.
With wrong side facing put
stitches of neckline on to the
same needles. Pick up 4 loops
from side of placket if
knitted. Tension 10. Knit
1 row. Cast off by one of
following methods:

1. Using latch tool –
   suitable for all except
   smallest garments.
2. Backstitching through
   loops of last row whilst
   garment hangs on
   needles.
3. Releasing on waste
   knitting (Tension 6) then
   backstitching as 2.

Sleeves

Knit 2 alike.
Arrange needles for 2 × 2 rib:

Children's and Ladies'
Sizes marked * increase

38*	38*	42	50	54	58	58*	62*	66	66*	70	70*	74	78	78*	82

1 stitch both ends to

38	40	44	50	54	58	60	64	66	68	70	72	74	78	80	82

Men's
Sizes marked * increase

66	70*	74	74*	78	78*	82	82*	86*	90	90*

1 stitch both ends to

68	70	74	76	78	80	82	84	88	90	92

Welt Cast on and knit as
before. Transfer stitches to
main bed. RC 000. Tension 6.
Knit in stocking stitch.

Children's and Ladies'
Increase at both ends by fully-
fashioned method every
following

5	5	6	7	8	8	8	9	8	7	7	7	6/7	6/7	6/7	6

rows. Number of times

9	11	11	11	11	12	14	14	16	19	20	20	21	21	23	24

Total stitches

56	62	66	72	76	82	88	92	98	106	110	112	116	120	126	130

Knit to RC

66	78	90	106	116	126	150	172	172	184	184	190	190	190	200	200

Men's Increase both ends
every following

8	9	10	9	8	8	8	8	7/8	7/8	7

rows. Number of times

12	14	14	16	19	20	20	21	21	23	24

Total stitches

92	98	102	108	116	120	122	126	130	136	140

Knit to RC

136	160	182	182	194	194	200	200	200	210	210

To Make Up If no placket has been knitted join left shoulder seam and neckband ends. For garments with placket sew 1 cm (½ inch) at shoulder end and make crocheted button loops along front shoulder opening and side of neckband. Sew on buttons. Sew cast off edges of sleeves to straight part of armholes. Fit sleeve into square armhole and sew into position. Seam sleeve and underarm seams.

TO RECAP

In this chapter you have learnt:

> *how to cast on and knit 2 × 2 ribbing*
> *how to knit a placket opening on a child's jumper*
> *how to knit and attach a round neckband...and...*

you have been given a basic jumper pattern in a wide range of sizes.

You could use the measurements given on the blocks to knit another jumper, perhaps adapting the pattern by knitting it in a stitch pattern. Make tension swatch, and either calculate pattern, or draw block on charter and knit to chart pattern. If you wish you could have 1 × 1 rib for welts and neckband. You would then start all pieces with an odd number of stitches, making the number right after knitting the welts.

This pattern has been written especially to show you how to adjust a standard pattern to make it suitable for men and women. In the men's sizes 10 rows and 10 stitches were added to the length and width of the sleeves. This meant that 6 rows needed to be added to the length from armhole cast off to shoulder shaping. I have left it for you to decide if you need any extra length in the body section.

6

FULLY-FASHIONED INCREASING AND DECREASING IN 2 BY 2 RIB: 2 BY 2 RIB RAGLAN SWEATER WITH A DOUBLE-THICKNESS ROUND NECKBAND

In this chapter your assignment is a 2 by 2 ribbed raglan sweater. The raglan decreasing will be fully-fashioned, and so will the increasing on the sleeves.

Fully-fashioned increasing and decreasing in rib stitches takes place inside the last group of main bed stitches. These are always left intact. The following series of diagrams and photographs shows clearly how to proceed.

INCREASING

```
              a b                 b a
   MB         | | o o | | o o | | o o | |
   RB         o o | | o o | | o o | | o o
```

2 by 2 ribbing

46

		a b										b a	
MB		| | h o o | | o o | | o o h | |
RB		o o o | | o o | | o o | | o o o

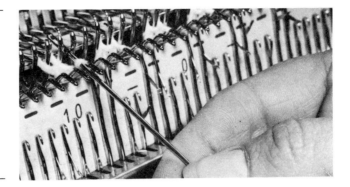

1ST INCREASE: *Stitches 'a b' have been moved 1 place outwards. A new stitch is being made at h on the left by putting the heel of the end rib bed stitch onto the main bed to fill the needle left empty. At the right you can see the completed group of 3 stitches on the main bed*

		a b c						c b a	
MB		| | h | o o | | o o | | o o | h | |
RB		o o o o | | o o | | o o | | o o o o

2ND INCREASE: *Stitches 'a b' have been moved 1 place outwards, and a new stitch is again made at the left on the main bed from the heel of stitch c. At the right you can see the completed group of 4 stitches on the main bed*

		a b c						c b a	
MB		| | o | | o o | | o o | | o o | | o | |
RB		o o h o o | | o o | | o o | | o o h o o

3RD INCREASE: *Stitches 'a b' have been moved 1 place outwards, and a new stitch is being made at letter h (left) on the rib bed from the heel of main bed stitch c. You see this completed at the right*

```
              a b                                    b a
MB    | | o o | | o o | | o o | | o o | | o o | |
RB    o o h | o o | | o o | | o o | | o o | h o o
              c                                      c
```

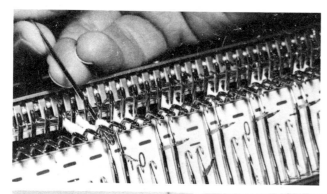

4TH INCREASE: *Stitches 'a b' have been moved 1 place outwards, and a new stitch is again being made at the left on the rib bed, this time from the heel of the end rib bed stitch c*

The sequence is completed with the stitches in the last diagram above in the same relative positions as in the first diagram, but with an increase of 4 stitches at both sides. In a garment several rows would be knitted between each increase

PRACTICE PIECE OF INCREASING

Cast on 30 stitches arranged for 2 × 2 rib. Knit the selvedge. RC 000. Tension 4../4... Knit 4 rows of rib. Increase fully-fashioned at both ends of the next row and every following 4th row, 8 times in all. RC 32. The sequence has been completed twice. There are 46 stitches. Leave on the needles.

Feel underneath the beds and find the edges of the knitting. It is beginning to curve inwards and feel slack. That is because it is now quite a lot wider than the cast on edge which is held firm by the comb and wire. If this slackness, or lack of tension, is not counteracted end stitches will begin to tuck instead of knitting. The remedy for this is to use the side weights as explained on Page 25, moving them up from time to time as the work becomes wider.

DECREASING

The numeral '2' indicates needles on which there are 2 stitches *after* decreasing.

```
       a b                           b a
MB   |  | o | | o o | | o o | | o o | | o | |
RB   o o 2 o o | | o o | | o o | | o o 2 o o
```

1ST DECREASE: *The left end rib bed stitch is being transferred in 1 place on rib bed to needle marked 2. The 2 stitches will be knitted together in the next row. Stitches 'a b' have been moved in 1 place*

DECREASE COMPLETED

```
       a b                          b a
MB   |  | 2 | o o | | o o | | o o | 2 | |
RB   o o o o | | o o | | o o | | o o o o
```

2ND DECREASE: *Another transfer from the rib bed to the main bed, to needle marked 2. Stitches 'a b' are moved in 1 place completing the decrease*

```
        a b                    b a
MB    | | 2 o o | | o o | | o o 2 | |
RB    o o o | | o o | | o o | | o o o
```

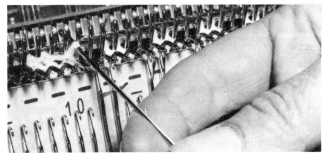

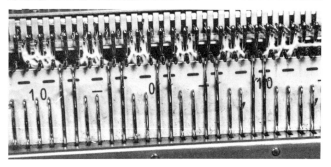

3RD DECREASE: *The 3rd main bed stitch is transferred to the 4th needle. Stitches 'a b' are moved in 1 place*

```
        a b                    b a
MB    | | o o | | o o | | o o | |
RB    o o 2 | o o | | o o | 2 o o
```

4TH DECREASE: *The third main bed stitch is transferred to the end rib bed needle. Back where we started. The sequence is complete*

PRACTICE PIECE OF DECREASING

Continue on the increasing sample by knitting 4 rows and then decreasing 1 stitch at both ends of the next row and every following 4th row 8 times in all. Knit 4 more rows. Cast off in rib.

When you knit the raglans in the pullover you will be using fully-fashioned decreasing. However, first you will cast off some stitches as you usually do when knitting any armhole. The number of stitches varies according to the size, and it does not always leave the end needles arranged as they are in the practice piece. Immediately after the casting off rearrange the end stitches so that there are at least 2 stitches at the ends on the main bed. There may be as many as 3 or 4 stitches, depending on how many were cast off, but there must be two in the 'a b' position you have practised, otherwise the seaming with the sleeve raglans will not look right. We need 'a b' stitches on all pieces so that in seaming by mattress stitching the 'a' stitches turn to the inside leaving a column of 'bb' between the decreasings.

TO KNIT THE JUMPER: RAGLAN STYLE: 2 BY 2 RIB THROUGHOUT

Knit a tension swatch in 2 by 2 rib using Tension 4../4... This is the tension given for the main parts of the jumper. Block out and measure as before stretching it as it will be stretched when worn. The measurements for the tension swatch used for garment shown on Pages 2, 5 and 6 were:

30 stitches and 40 rows = 10 cm (4 inches)

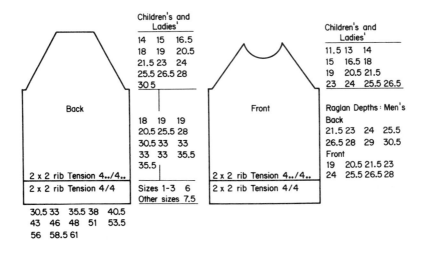

NOTES: Raglan depths on sleeves are same as back and front.

Lengths given for back and front are for children's and ladies' garments. Adjust length for men's garments. The wrong side is facing as the garment is knitted.

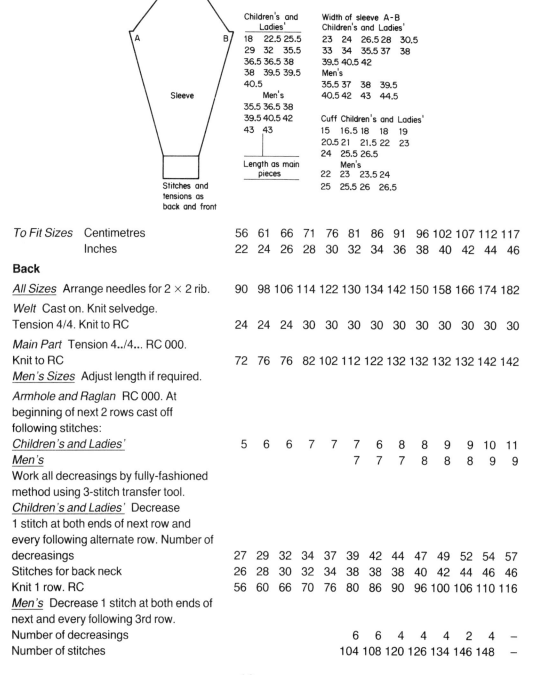

Children's and Ladies'
18 22.5 25.5
29 32 35.5
36.5 36.5 38
38 39.5 39.5
40.5

Men's
35.5 36.5 38
39.5 40.5 42
43 43

Length as main pieces

Width of sleeve A-B
Children's and Ladies'
23 24 26.5 28 30.5
33 34 35.5 37 38
39.5 40.5 42

Men's
35.5 37 38 39.5
40.5 42 43 44.5

Cuff Children's and Ladies'
15 16.5 18 18 19
20.5 21 21.5 22 23
24 25.5 26.5

Men's
22 23 23.5 24
25 25.5 26 26.5

A   B   Sleeve

Stitches and tensions as back and front

To Fit Sizes	Centimetres	56	61	66	71	76	81	86	91	96	102	107	112	117
	Inches	22	24	26	28	30	32	34	36	38	40	42	44	46

Back

All Sizes Arrange needles for 2 × 2 rib.

	90	98	106	114	122	130	134	142	150	158	166	174	182

Welt Cast on. Knit selvedge.
Tension 4/4. Knit to RC

	24	24	24	30	30	30	30	30	30	30	30	30	30

Main Part Tension 4../4... RC 000.
Knit to RC

	72	76	76	82	102	112	122	132	132	132	132	142	142

Men's Sizes Adjust length if required.

Armhole and Raglan RC 000. At beginning of next 2 rows cast off following stitches:

Children's and Ladies'	5	6	6	7	7	7	6	8	8	9	9	10	11
Men's						7	7	7	8	8	8	9	9

Work all decreasings by fully-fashioned method using 3-stitch transfer tool.
Children's and Ladies' Decrease 1 stitch at both ends of next row and every following alternate row. Number of decreasings

	27	29	32	34	37	39	42	44	47	49	52	54	57

Stitches for back neck

	26	28	30	32	34	38	38	38	40	42	44	46	46

Knit 1 row. RC

	56	60	66	70	76	80	86	90	96	100	106	110	116

Men's Decrease 1 stitch at both ends of next and every following 3rd row.
Number of decreasings

						6	6	4	4	4	2	4	–

Number of stitches

						104	108	120	126	134	146	148	–

Knit 2 rows. RC   20 20 14 14 14 8 14 –

Decrease 1 stitch at both ends of next and every following alternate row.

Number of decreasings   33 35 41 43 46 51 51 59

Stitches remaining for back neck   38 38 38 40 42 44 46 46

Knit 1 row. RC   86 90 96 100 106 110 116 120

All Sizes   Transfer stitches to main bed. Release on waste knitting

Front

All Sizes   Knit as back to armhole. RC 000.

Children's and Ladies'   Knit as back to RC*   30 34 38 42 48   52 58 62 68 72 78 82 88

Number of stitches   52 54 58 60 62   66 66 66 68 70 72 74 74

Men's   Knit as back to RC**   56 60 66 70 76 80 86 90

Number of stitches   68 68 68 70 72 74 76 76

Divide for Neck   by putting given number of centre stitches into holding position on main bed, transferring from rib bed. Put stitches left of centre into holding position. It is easier to hold stitches on main bed. Set main carriage to hold. Remove comb and weights. Rehang comb on stitches at right. Use shortest comb, and fewer weights.

All Sizes   Stitches at centre   10 12 12 14 16 14 14 14 16 18 20 22 22

Shape neck by putting stitches at neck edge into holding position on alternate rows always when carriage is at raglan edge. Wrap inside needles.

Children's and Ladies'   Stitches to holding position on alternate rows   4 stitches all sizes

then   2 2 2 2 2   Sizes 6–13 2 stitches 4 times

then 1 stitch every row following number of times   5 5 6 6 6   Sizes 6–13 3

AT SAME TIME decrease 1 stitch at raglan edge on alternate rows following number of times   8 8 9 9 9   Sizes 6–13 9

Put remaining 2 stitches to holding position. RC   46 50 56 60 66   70 76 80 86 90 96 100 106

Men's   Stitches to holding position on alternate rows   Sizes 6–13 4 stitches once

then   2 stitches 3 times

then 1 stitch every row   5 times

AT SAME TIME decrease 1 stitch at raglan edge on alternate rows following number of times   Sizes 6–13 10

53

Put remaining 2 stitches to holding position. RC

					76	80	86	90	96	100	106	110

All Sizes Fasten off yarn. Take carriage to left. Leave centre group of stitches in holding position. Transfer stitches of left side for rib. Reset RC to start of neck shaping * or **. Knit left side reversing shapings. All stitches are in holding position on main bed. Release on waste knitting.

Total stitches decreased front neck												
36	38	40	42	44	48	48	48	50	52	54	56	56

Sleeves

Knit 2 alike. Arrange needles for 2 × 2 rib.

Children's and Ladies'												
42*	46*	50*	50*	58	62	62*	62*	66*	66*	74	74	74*

Men's												
					66	70	70*	74	74*	74*	74*	78

Welt Knit as before at tension 4/4.

Main Part Tension 4../4... RC 000. Sizes marked * Increase 1 stitch fully-fashioned at both ends before knitting 1st row.

Children's and Ladies' Increase 1 stitch fully-fashioned both ends every rows following number of times

5	6	7	7	7	7	7	6	7	6	7	6	6
12	12	13	15	16	18	19	21	20	22	21	23	24

Number of stitches

68	72	78	82	90	98	102	106	108	112	116	120	124

RC

60	72	91	105	112	126	133	126	140	132	147	138	144

Knit straight to RC (adjust if required)

70	90	100	116	126	140	146	146	150	150	156	156	160

Men's Increase fully-fashioned both ends every rows the following number of times

					7	7	7	7	7	6	6	6
					19	19	20	21	22	25	26	27

Number of stitches

					106	108	112	116	120	124	128	132

RC

					133	133	140	147	154	150	156	162

Knit straight to RC (adjust if required)

					140	146	150	156	160	166	170	170

Armhole and Raglan RC 000. Decrease fully-fashioned as before.

Children's and Ladies' At beginning of next 2 rows cast off

5	6	6	7	7	7	6	8	8	9	9	10	11

Decrease 1 stitch both ends of next and every following 3rd row following number of times

8	10	14	16	14	14	14	18	22	24	26	28	32

Number of stitches

42	40	38	36	48	56	62	54	48	46	46	44	38

Knit 2 rows. RC

26	32	44	50	44	44	44	56	68	74	80	86	98

Decrease 1 stitch both ends of next and every following alternate row following number of times

10	9	6	5	11	13	16	12	9	8	8	7	4

| Number of stitches | 22 | 22 | 26 | 26 | 26 | 30 | all sizes |

Knit 1 row. RC — 46 50 56 60 66 70 76 80 86 90 96 100 106

Men's At beginning of next 2 rows cast off — 7 7 7 8 8 8 9 9

Decrease 1 stitch both ends of next and every following 3rd row following number of times — 12 14 16 18 20 20 24 24

Number of stitches — 68 66 66 64 64 68 62 66

Knit 2 rows RC — 38 44 50 56 62 62 74 74

Decrease 1 stitch both ends of next and every following alternate row following number of times — 19 18 18 17 17 19 16 18

Number of stitches — 30 all sizes

Knit 1 row. RC — 76 80 86 90 96 100 106 110

Sleeve Top

All Sizes Put into holding position following stitches at left first transferring them to main bed — 8 8 12 12 12 16 all sizes

Continue to decrease raglan at right on alternate rows 5 more times. AT SAME TIME shape left by putting into holding position on main bed.

All Sizes 4 stitches once, 1 stitch 3 times. Wrap inside needles.

Children's and Ladies' RC — 56 60 66 70 76 80 86 90 96 100 106 110 116

Men's RC — 86 90 96 100 106 110 116 120

Put remaining 2 stitches to holding position.

All Sizes Total stitches remaining — 17 17 21 21 21 25 all sizes

Release remaining stitches on waste knitting. Reverse sleeve top on second sleeve.

Neckband

Before knitting neckband sew up 3 raglan seams. The 4th is either sewn up after attaching neckband or turned into placket opening. Placket should be on a front raglan, and should be knitted before neckband. Allow 4 extra stitches on neckband to attach to side of placket. This is a double neckband. Arrange needles on main bed only:

All Sizes Number of stitches — 98 102 114 118 122 138 138 138 142 146 150 154 154

Tension 6. Waste yarn. Cast on. Knit 6 rows. Knit 1 row with nylon cord to make it easier to remove waste knitting.

Main yarn. Knit 3 rows. RC 000. Transfer
stitches for 2 × 2 rib. Hang comb and
weights taking care not to split stitches.

*Turning up double neckband: 6 rows of waste, 1 row with nylon cord, 3 rows main yarn
have been knitted on main bed. Stitches have been transferred for rib. The bed has been
lowered 1 position to make it easier to insert comb. Notice knit side of main bed stitches on
rib bed*

Knit in rib, 4 rows at each of the following   3../3.. 3./3.   3/3
tensions: 3/3   3./3. 3../3.. RC 24

*Transfer rib stitches to main
bed. Rib bed has been lowered.
Remove comb and weights,
taking care stitches do not
spring off*

*Pick up heels from 1st row of
rib bed stitches and place them
on needles to which last row
of rib bed stitches were
transferred. Tension 6. Knit
3 rows*

Pick up loops of first row of stocking stitch and place on needles

Tension 8. Knit 1 row

Wrong side facing, place neckline stitches of garment on same needles, noting that 2 stitches at each end of neckband are placed on same needle.

To Make Up   If placket is required, pick up loops on sleeve edge of raglan including neckband for part or whole of length. Measure edge and calculate stitches at rate of 30 stitches = 10 cm knitting in stocking stitch at tension 6. Wrong side of sleeve facing, pick up required number of stitches from edge. Knit 6 rows tension 6, 1 row tension 8, 6 rows tension 6. Pick up loops of first row to make hem. Cast off. Finish other edge with buttonhole loops as in previous pattern. If no placket is required seam 4th raglan. Join ends of neckband. Sew underarm and side seams.

MORE ABOUT INCREASING AND DECREASING IN 2 BY 2 RIB
If you should decide to knit a 2 × 2 jumper with a set in sleeve, and there are a good many patterns about, you will need to organise a different end needle

arrangement from the one you have just used, once you reach the armhole shaping.

We always have to think about seaming the garment together, and it is too late to plan how you will do it when the knitting is finished. If you take the end arrangement you have just used:

```
MB    | | o o | | o o | |
RB    o o | | o o | | o o
```

you will lose the end stitch when you sew the sleeve into the armhole, and be left with a column of single stitches up to the shoulder.

The arrangement you need is:

```
MB    | | | o o | | o o | | |
RB    o o o | | o o | | o o o
```

You may have to adjust the number of stitches you cast off at the armhole to get this right, but with a little thought beforehand the appearance of the garment can be much improved.

TO RECAP

In this chapter you have learnt:

>*how to do fully-fashioned increasing and decreasing in 2 × 2 rib*
>*how to knit a garment entirely in rib*
>*how to knit a different type of round neckband...and...*

you have now been given a raglan pattern in a wide range of sizes.

You could use the facts and figures of this pattern for knitting another jumper in the same yarn in stocking stitch. The tension swatch in the last chapter measured the same as the 2 × 2 rib in this chapter.

7

ANOTHER NEEDLE ARRANGEMENT
FOR 2 BY 2 RIBBING: 2 PLY VEE-NECK RAGLAN PULLOVER
WITH WELTS AND NECKBAND IN THIS RIB

The ribs knitted in the previous chapters look very attractive in average weight yarns. If finer yarns are used they are not necessarily suitable. There is another needle layout for 2 by 2 rib which is better for this purpose. In this chapter it will be used for the welts and neckband for a Vee-neck pullover to be knitted either in 2 ply yarn or in 2 strands of industrial acrylic.

CASTING ON AND KNITTING TENSION SWATCH
1. Rib bed in half pitch. Set racking handle to position 5.
2. Select needles.

```
MB   | | o | | o | | o | |
RB     o | | o | | o | | o
```

3. Align needles.
4. Thread main yarn.
5. Zig zag row. Rack to 4 (Jones + Brother and Knitmaster), 6 (Toyota).

```
MB   | | o | | o | | o | |
RB   † o | | o | | o | |
```

Bring an extra needle on the rib bed to working position at '†' to complete zig zag.
6. Hang comb.
7. Rack back to 5 and transfer extra rib bed loop before knitting 3 selvedge rows at tension used for zig zag.
     Tension 0/0, or below 0 if possible as it is on some machines, using main yarn knit 1 row.
8. The beginning of ribbing can be improved by increasing the tension

gradually for the first few rows until the full rib tension is reached. If this is done an extra 2 or 4 rows are knitted to compensate. The rib for this garment will be knitted at Tension 1./1.. Knit 1 row at each of the following tensions: 0./0. 0../0.. 1/1.

Set the Tension to 1./1. and knit 7 rows. This counts as 8 rows altogether. Change to waste yarn. Knit 6 rows. RC 000. Main yarn. Knit 60 rows. As length measurement only is required it is not necessary to mark 21st stitches. Change to waste yarn. Knit 8 rows. Release from machine.

9. Examine the selvedge and the first few rows. Knitting it this way takes a little more time and trouble, but the appearance makes it worth doing. Block out and rest fabric pinning out as before. After resting measure length.

The measurement of the swatch used for the garment shown on Pages 2, 5 and 7 was:

$$48 \text{ rows} = 10 \text{ cm (4 inches)}$$

10. Knit a stocking stitch tension swatch using Tension 4. The measurements of the swatch used in the garment were:

$$36 \text{ stitches and } 52 \text{ rows} = 10 \text{ cm (4 inches)}$$

FURTHER IMPROVEMENTS IN CASTING ON
These are ways in which the zig zag row can be further improved. This is particularly important when using fine yarn.

a) Jones + Brother machines only: Set the slide lever at the bottom of the rib carriage to position II (see picture on Page 61). This has the effect of raising the rib bed needles to a higher position on the needle bed. In this way the thread of the zig zag row is shortened. This can be used alone, or with either of the following two methods.

b) Before knitting the zig zag set the rib carriage to hold and push all the rib bed needles to be used to holding position. Knit the zig zag row. The yarn will form loops on the main bed, and will pass outside the stems of the rib bed needles, considerably shortening the amount of yarn used.
The first selvedge row must be knitted on the rib bed, in order to return those needles to working position. This means reversing the setting of the carriages for the circular rows, so that the rib bed knits

Zig zag row knitted with most rib bed needles in holding position. At the right are a few in the more usual position, showing the difference in the length of the zig zag threads

the first and third rows and slips the second row, and the main bed does the opposite. Before starting to knit the selvedge release the holding cam lever on the rib bed.

c) On the Jones + Brother 850 ribber there is a knob on the connecting pin which joins the two carriages together. The instruction book recommends putting the yarn into the yarn feed and then passing it anti-clockwise round the pin before knitting the row. This has the effect of shortening the zig zag thread. In machines without this knob tie the yarn to the clamp and thread in the usual way. Hold the tip of the right forefinger against the joined carriages with the yarn running round it anti-clockwise. Knit the row using the left hand to move the carriage.

Try out these methods on practice pieces, and use the one which you think gives the best result whenever you knit either form of 2 by 2 rib.

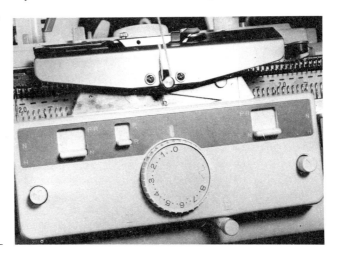

Yarn tightening Jones + Brother 850

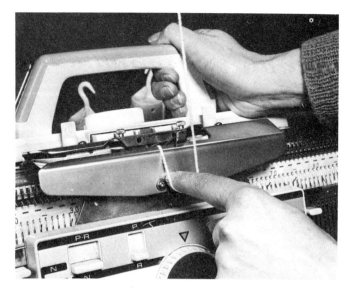

COUNTING THE NEEDLES IN USE: WHAT THE PATTERN MEANS

Different wording is used in this pattern for the selection of needles. Let us take as an example the smallest size in the pattern. When the welt for the back has been knitted and the stitches have been transferred, there will be 107 stitches on the main bed. The welt is said to be 'over the width of 107 main bed needles'. In this needle setting for 2 × 2 rib, two out of every three needles on both beds will be in work.

As an experiment push 107 main bed needles into working position and then arrange them as they would be for the type of rib you have just knitted. Set the rib bed to half pitch, and arrange needles to complete the rib setting. There are 72 needles in working position on the main bed and 70 on the rib bed; a total of 142 stitches over the width of 107 main bed needles. The difference between 107 and 142 is the number of extra stitches which will be knitted in the rib using this setting. The extra stitches in the same width is what makes this setting so much more suitable for fine yarns. Knitted in 1 by 1 rib, or the other form of 2 by 2, there would only be 107 stitches. In fine yarns ribs knitted in full pitch often look as if they have ladders beside the columns of stitches.

In this form of 2 by 2 rib, which is sometimes known as '2 up 1 down', that is 2 needles 'up' in working position and 1 'down' in non-working position, the needle width on the main bed must be divisible by 3 plus 2 extra needles to make the ends match. In the other form of 2 by 2 rib the needle width is divisible by 4 plus 2 extra needles.

FULLY-FASHIONED INCREASING AND DECREASING

The method is similar to the one given in the previous chapter, but must take account of the extra stitches in the width of the work. Cast on over the width of 29 main bed needles. Follow the series of diagrams and make a similar sample to the last one, knitting 4 rows before increasing, and 4 rows between each increase. Knit through the sequence twice.

```
          a b              b a
MB        | | o | | o | | o | |
RB          o | | o | | o | | o
```

2 × 2 ribbing – '2 up 1 down'

```
          a b                  b a
MB        | | h o | | o | | o h | |
RB          o o | | o | | o | | o o
```

1ST INCREASE: Stitches 'a b' are moved out one place and the spaces filled by picking up the heels of the nearest rib bed stitches

```
          a b                    b a
MB     | | | h o | | o | | o h | | |
RB     o o o | | o | | o | | o o o
```

2ND INCREASE: Same procedure as in the first increase. Now there are 4 main bed stitches together. Make sure those stitches knit correctly by pushing the needles to holding position.

```
          a b                       b a
MB     | | o | | o | | o | | o | | o | |
RB     o h h o | | o | | o | | o h h
```

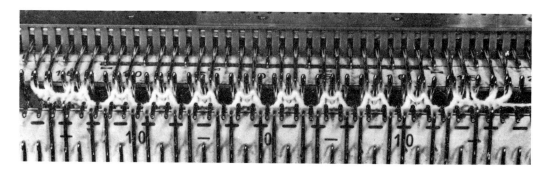

3RD INCREASE: This increase is 1 needle place both sides on the main bed. This time there are no extra stitches on that bed; 2 stitches are needed on the rib bed to keep the rib formation correct. These are formed by picking up heels from the nearest main bed stitches

Notice that this sequence, which is now complete, only gives an increase of 3 main bed needle places at both sides. A pair of rib bed stitches is only equal to one empty needle on the main bed. That is why we have to increase two stitches on the rib bed in the same row. The same thing applies when decreasing. Working through the increasing sequence once, as in the photographs, gives an increase of 6 main bed needle places, counting as 6 stitches. For practice work through twice. The knitting will now be over the width of 41 main bed needles.

Sarah wearing the pixie hat (Chapter 2), legwarmers (Chapter 4), and circular-knitted scarf (Chapter 9). For extra warmth on Uncle Laurie's boat she is carrying a hot water bottle in a circular-knitted cover (Chapter 9)

Marion, mother of baby Paul, wearing a Fisherman's rib overtop (Chapter 3)

Twins, Edward and Simon, wearing pullovers featured in Chapter 5

Carol modelling the skinny rib pullover from Chapter 6

Sue wearing the fine-knit pullover from Chapter 7

Carol with a 2 by 2 rib cardigan (Chapter 8) to match the jumper

Baby Paul in a circular-knitted jumper from Chapter 9

Laurie, casually dressed for sailing. The tee-shirt is in Chapter 10

Ruby looking elegant in the suit from Chapters 11 and 12

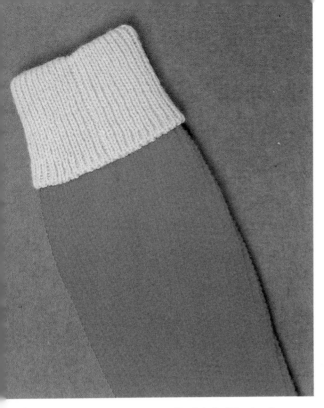

Sew a fine seam: Decreasing in English rib (Chapter 4)

Mattress stitching stocking stitch with fully-fashioned increasing (sleeves of garment in Chapter 7)

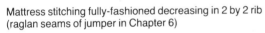

Mattress stitching fully-fashioned decreasing in 2 by 2 rib (raglan seams of jumper in Chapter 6)

Mattress stitching a straight seam in 2 by 2 rib, keeping correct rib formation (side seam of jumper in Chapter 6)

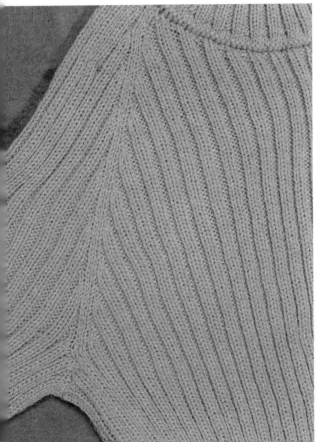

Single-thickness round neckband from Chapter 5

Double-thickness round neckband from Chapter 6

Vee-neckband showing mitre from Chapter 7

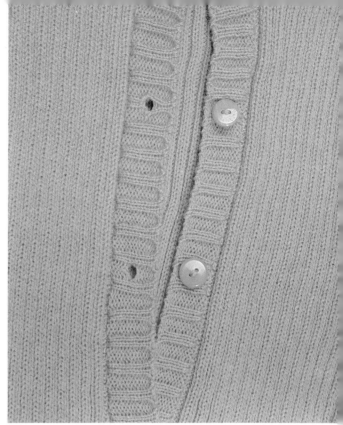

Buttonholes from Chapter 8

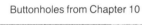

Buttonholes from Chapter 10

Button and buttonholes from Chapter 12

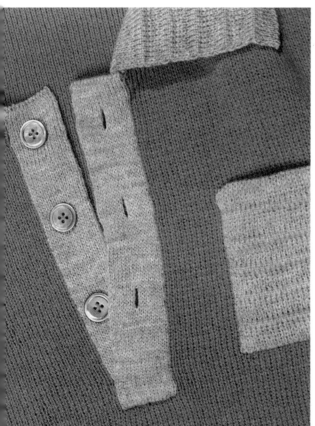

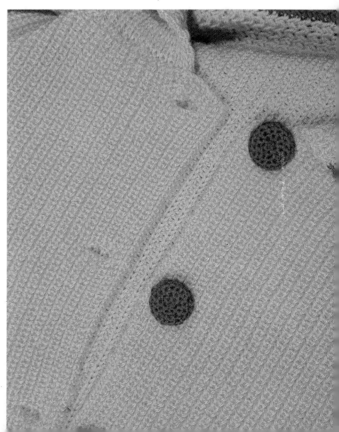

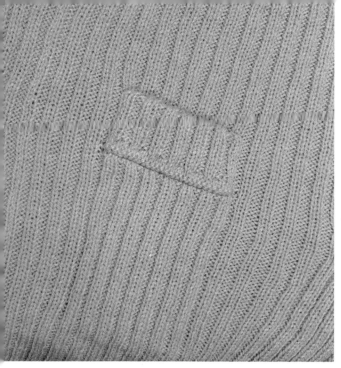

Pocket heading from Chapter 8

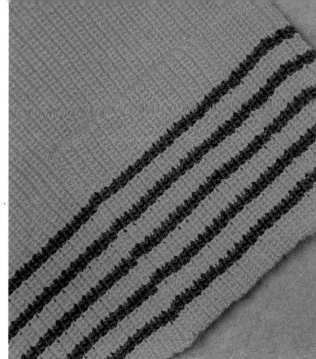

Pocket from Chapter 12

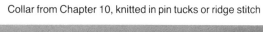

Collar from Chapter 10, knitted in pin tucks or ridge stitch

Collar from Chapter 12, knitted in racked English rib

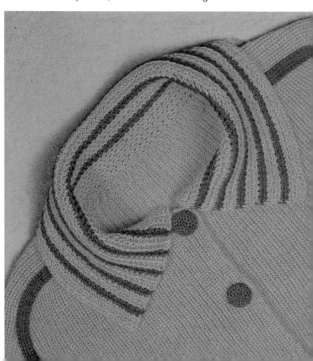

Now continue with decreasing.

```
      a b    *             *    b a
MB    | | o | | o | | o | | o | | o | |
RB      o | | o | | o | | o | | o | | o
```

```
      a b                       b a
MB    | | 3 | o | | o | | o | | o | 3 | |
RB      o o o | | o | | o | | o | o o o
```

*1ST DECREASE: All decreased stitches are placed on the 3rd working needles from the edge. Here 2 stitches have been removed from the rib bed and are placed together onto the needles marked * in previous diagram. Stitches 'a b' are moved in 1 place*

```
      a b                 b a
MB    | | 2 o | | o | | o 2 | |
RB      o o | | o | | o | | o o
```

2ND DECREASE: The 3rd stitches from the end on the main bed have been transferred to the 4th needle from the end. Stitches 'a b' are moved in 1 place

65

```
        a b          b a
MB   | | o | | o | | o | |
RB   o 2 | o | | o | 2 o
```

3RD DECREASE: The 3rd stitches from the ends on the main bed have been transferred to the end working needles of the rib bed. Stitches 'a b' are moved in 1 place

This ends the decreasing sequence. Working through it twice will bring the work back to the width of 29 main bed needles as in the beginning.

TO KNIT VEE-NECKED PULLOVER

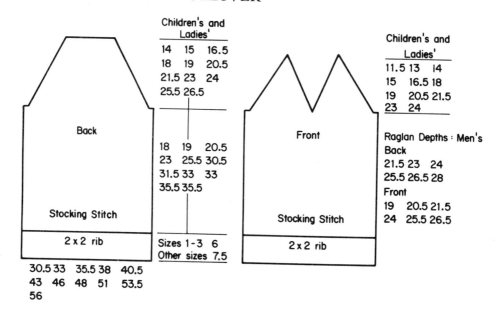

Children's and Ladies'

14   15   16.5
18   19   20.5
21.5 23   24
25.5 26.5

18   19   20.5
23   25.5 30.5
31.5 33   33
35.5 35.5

Sizes 1-3 6
Other sizes 7.5

Back — Stocking Stitch — 2 x 2 rib

30.5 33 35.5 38 40.5
43   46 48   51 53.5
56

Children's and Ladies'

11.5 13   14
15   16.5 18
19   20.5 21.5
23   24

Raglan Depths : Men's
Back
21.5 23   24
25.5 26.5 28
Front
19   20.5 21.5
24   25.5 26.5

Front — Stocking Stitch — 2 x 2 rib

NOTE : Raglan depths on sleeves are the same as on back and front.

Lengths given for back and front are for children's and ladies' garments. Adjust length for men's garments.

66

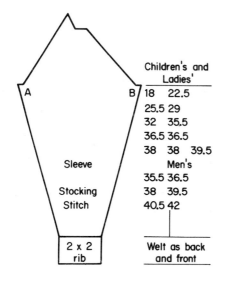

Sleeve

Stocking
Stitch

2 x 2
rib

Children's and Ladies'
18   22.5
25.5 29
32 35.5
36.5 36.5
38 38 39.5
Men's
35.5 36.5
38 39.5
40.5 42

Welt as back
and front

Width of sleeve A-B
Children's and Ladies'
23 24 26.5 28 30.5
33 34 35.5 37 38
39.5
Men's
35.5 37 38 39.5 40.5
42

Cuff Children's and Ladies'
15 16.5 18 18 19
20.5 21 21.5 22 23 24
Men's
22 23 23 5 24 25 25.5

To Fit Chest/Bust Sizes											
Centimetres	56	61	66	71	76	81	86	91	97	102	107
Inches	22	24	26	28	30	32	34	36	38	40	42

Back

Welt Over width of
main bed needles arrange needles of both
beds for 2 × 2 ribbing; 2 up 1 down setting.
Using main yarn cast on. Knit selvedge and first
3 rows of rib as in tension swatch. RC 000. Knit
to RC

107	116	125	134	143	152	161	170	179	188	197
30	30	30	36	36	36	36	36	36	36	36

Transfer all stitches to main bed. Do this as
follows for good appearance on right side.
Transfer each pair of rib bed needles to opposite
empty main bed needles, always transferring
either left or right stitch of each pair first, not
sometimes one then the other.

Main Part Increase 1 or 2 stitches, except sizes
6, 10 to give following stitches
Tension 4. RC 000. Knit in stocking stitch to RC
Adjust length to individual requirements. Men's
sizes: 30−50 rows longer with separate
instructions for armhole and raglan.

108	118	126	136	144	152	162	172	180	188	198
98	106	112	126	140	168	176	182	182	196	196

Armhole and Raglan Shaping RC 000.
All Sizes At beginning next 2 rows cast off
following stitches
Using 3-stitch transfer tool decrease 1 stitch
fully-fashioned at both ends of next and every
following 3rd row:

6	7	8	9	9	8	8	9	9	9	10

	1	2	3	4	5	6	7	8	9	10	11
Children's and Ladies' Number of times	6	6	6	8	8	10	8	6	8	8	6
Number of stitches	84	92	98	102	110	116	130	142	146	154	166
Knit 2 rows RC	20	20	20	26	26	32	26	20	26	26	20
Men's Number of times						16	14	14	14	14	12
Number of stitches						104	118	126	134	142	154
Knit 2 rows RC						50	44	44	44	44	38

All Sizes Decrease 1 stitch at both ends of next and every following alternate row:

	1	2	3	4	5	6	7	8	9	10	11
Children's and Ladies' Number of times	26	29	32	33	36	36	42	48	49	52	58
RC	72	78	84	92	98	104	110	116	124	130	136
Men's Number of times						30	36	40	43	46	52
RC						110	116	124	130	136	142
All Sizes Number of stitches for back neck	32	34	34	36	38	44	46	46	48	50	50

Release on waste knitting.

NOTE Back neck in adult sizes can be shaped using holding position dividing as for front neck as follows:

	1	2	3	4	5	6	7	8	9	10	11
Ladies' Divide at RC						96	102	108	116	122	128
Men's Divide at RC						102	108	116	122	128	134

Leaving 14 stitches at right in working position push remainder to holding position. Continuing to shape raglan 4 more times at right knit 2 rows. On next row and every following alternate row push 4, then 3, then 2 stitches to holding position at left, always wrapping inside needle. Push remaining 2 stitches to holding position. Repeat at left reversing shapings. Release on waste knitting. Back neck stitches are as given for straight back neckline.

Front

Knit as back to armhole and raglan shaping.

Armhole and Raglan Shaping RC 000.

All Sizes decrease as for back dividing for neck at:

	1	2	3	4	5	6	7	8	9	10	11
Children's and Ladies' RC	4	6	2	6	8	6	8	8	6	8	10
Men's RC						6	4	10	10	10	14

Set carriage to hold. Put all stitches left of centre to holding position. Continuing to shape raglan at right, decrease 1 stitch at neck edge:

	1	2	3	4	5	6	7	8	9	10	11
Children's and Ladies' Following row intervals	3/2	3/2	3	3	3	3	3	3	4/3	4/3	4/3
Number of times	22	23	23	24	25	28	29	29	30	31	31
Knit to RC	60	66	72	80	86	92	98	104	112	118	124
Men's Following row intervals						4/3	4/3	4/3	4/3	4/3	4/3
Number of times as Ladies'											
Knit to RC						98	106	112	118	124	130

Fasten off yarn. Take carriage to left. Set carriage to knit back. Reset RC

Knit left front reversing shapings.

Sleeves

Knit 2 alike.
Over width of following front bed needles arrange needles of both beds for rib:

	1	2	3	4	5	6	7	8	9	10	11
Children's and Ladies'	53*	56*	62*	62*	68	71*	74	74*	80	80*	86
Men's						77*	80	83*	86	86*	92

Cast on and knit welt as before. Transfer stitches to main bed. Increase 1 or 2 stitches in sizes marked * to give:

	1	2	3	4	5	6	7	8	9	10	11
Children's and Ladies'	54†	58	64†	64	68	72†	74†	76	80	82	86
Men's						78	80	84	86	88	92†

All Sizes Tension 4. RC 000. Using 2-stitch transfer tool increase fully-fashioned 1 stitch at both ends of 4th row on sizes marked † then on all sizes at following intervals

	1	2	3	4	5	6	7	8	9	10	11
(intervals)	7	8	8	8	8	8	7	7	7	7	7
Children's and Ladies' Number of times	12	14	15	18	19	21	24	25	25	26	27
Number of stitches	80	86	96	100	108	116	122	126	130	134	140
Knit straight to RC	92	118	130	150	164	182	188	188	194	194	202
Men's Number of times						24	25	25	27	28	28
Number of stitches						126	130	134	140	144	150
Knit straight to RC						182	188	194	202	208	214

Shape Raglan RC 000.
At beginning of next 2 rows cast off following stitches:

	1	2	3	4	5	6	7	8	9	10	11
All Sizes	6	7	8	9	9	8	8	9	9	9	10

Using 3-stitch transfer tool decrease 1 stitch fully-fashioned at both ends of next and every following 3rd row:

	1	2	3	4	5	6	7	8	9	10	11
Children's and Ladies' Number of times	18	20	18	24	22	18	18	22	26	28	30
Number of stitches remaining	32	32	44	34	46	64	70	64	60	60	60
Knit 2 rows RC	56	62	56	74	68	56	56	68	80	86	92
Men's Number of times						14	16	22	22	24	30
Number of stitches remaining						82	82	72	78	78	70
Knit 2 rows RC						44	50	68	68	74	92

Decrease 1 stitch at both ends of next and every following alternate row:

	1	2	3	4	5	6	7	8	9	10	11
Children's and Ladies' Number of times	2	2	8	3	9	18	21	18	16	16	16
Number of stitches	28 all sizes										
Knit 1 row RC	60	66	72	80	86	92	98	104	112	118	124
Men's Number of times						27	27	22	25	25	21
Number of stitches						28 all sizes					
Knit 1 row. RC						98	104	112	118	124	134

All Sizes Put 10 stitches at left into holding position. Set carriage to hold. Continue to

decrease 1 stitch on raglan at right on alternate
rows 6 more times. AT SAME TIME, starting on
3rd row, put stitches to holding position on
alternate rows as follows. 4 2 2 2, remembering
to wrap inside needles.

Children's and Ladies' RC	72	78	84	92	98	104	110	116	124	130	136
Men's RC						110	116	124	130	136	146

There are 22 stitches remaining. Release on
waste knitting.

Neckband in 2 × 2 rib with mitre at centre. Before
knitting and attaching neckband join up all raglan
seams. In all sizes neckbands join at the mitred
centre front. In ladies' sizes 7–11, and in all men's
sizes there is also a join centre back, so 2
half-length neckband pieces are knitted.

Whole Neckbands Over width of	137	146	161	167	173	188

front bed needles arrange needles of both beds
for 2 × 2 rib. Cast on as for welts. Knit 14 rows of
rib. 6 rows at Tension 0../0..; 4 rows at Tension
1/1; 4 rows at Tension 1./1.. AT THE SAME
TIME on 2nd and every following alternate row
6 times in all make mitre by increasing 1 stitch
at both ends. Changing tension makes band lie
flat. Do not use fully-fashioned method. Keep rib
formation correct.

Half Neckbands Knit 2 pieces.
Ladies' Over width of following front bed
needles

Men's Over width of following front bed needles	–	98	104	107	110	116
	98	107	107	113	116	119

cast on as for welts. Knit as for whole neckbands
increasing at 1 end only, right on 1st piece, left
on 2nd piece.

All Bands Fill intermediate needles of both beds
from heels of stitches opposite. Set carriages for
circular knitting. Make certain there are the same
number of stitches on both beds. Tension 4/4;
knit 8 rows (4 rows on each bed). Transfer
stitches to main bed (2 stitches to a needle).
Tension 6; knit 1 row. Put markers into the last
row to indicate number of back neck stitches and
22 both sides for sleeve tops.

Joining Garment to Band *Whole Bands*. With this type of Vee-neck band it is not possible to join it
all on at the same time. Hold garment wrong side facing. Starting a *right* of band, put *left* neck edge
onto needles. There will be approximately 2 needles for every 3 rows knitted on front. Keep to a
straight line of stitches. Put stitches of sleeve top and half back neck on needles from markers to
centre. Set machine to slip. Needles in working position. Push needles of right half to upper working

position. Tension 10; knit 1 row. Only needles with band and garment on will knit. Cast off with latch tool leaving last loop on needle right of centre. All needles in working position. Carriage still in slip. Move carriage to right. Put other half of back neck, other sleeve top and right neck edge on needles left of centre. Bring all needles to upper working position except last one at right. Knit 1 row. Cast off with latch tool starting with stitch at right.

Half Bands

Piece 1. Join left edge, sleeve top, half back neck to band, centre front neck opening at right.
Piece 2. Join right edge, sleeve top, half back neck to band, centre front neck opening at left.

To Make Up   Seam ends of neckband. Sew underarm and sleeve seams.

TO RECAP

In this chapter you have learnt:

> *how to knit the '2 up 1 down' version of 2 by 2 rib*
> *how to make a really good beginning to a piece of ribbing*
> *how to shape the back neckline*
> *how to knit and attach a ribbed Vee-neck band...and...*

you have now been given a raglan pattern for fine yarn in as wide a range of sizes as the width of the needle bed will allow.

8

POCKETS AND BUTTONHOLES IN RIB: CARDIGAN IN 2 BY 2 RIBBING

This chapter shows you how to knit a ribbed cardigan. The new techniques needed concern the knitting of pockets, buttonholes and front bands.

It is also helpful to know how to turn the jumper pattern in Chapter 6 into a pattern for a cardigan. The same method can then be used to knit cardigans to team up with any jumpers you knit.

POCKETS FOR A RIBBED CARDIGAN

The pocket linings and headings are knitted first, and released on waste knitting. The first thing to do, therefore, is to decide on the width of the pocket. Between a quarter and a third of the width of the front is about right. The length is usually a little more than the width. In ribbed garments a 'bag pocket' (double length) is not necessary because the sewing down at the sides and bottom does not show.

The fronts are then knitted as far as the pocket opening position, which is the same number of rows as the linings. Next the pocket position in the width of the front has to be decided. The following arrangement is an acceptable way of doing that:

Subtract Pocket stitches from Front stitches. Divide remainder by 4. Arrange as shown here:

← Armhole   Centre →
← ¼ of Remainder → : ← Pocket width → : ← ¾ of Remainder →

Having knitted the front up to the pocket opening position, transfer all the stitches of the pocket width as follows:

a) to main bed if the right side of garment is facing
b) to rib bed if the wrong side is facing, as it will be in the cardigan in this chapter

Stitches of the pocket heading are placed on the same needles, right sides together, and cast off together by hand – a little more tricky on the rib bed than on the main bed, but it can be done with care and patience.

The pocket lining stitches are placed on the needles to replace those cast off. They are transferred for rib, and the knitting is continued. The pocket is complete except for sewing lining and heading into position.

PRACTICE POCKET IN 2 BY 2 RIB

For practice we are going to knit a small pocket. All those in the pattern are knitted in exactly the same way. The double thickness pocket heading in 2 by 2 rib is knitted by the method used for the neckband of the jumper in Chapter 6, except that the tension remains 4/4 for all the rib.

Pocket Heading

Bring 18 main bed needles to working position. Tension 6. Using waste yarn cast on and knit 6 rows. Knit 1 row with the nylon cord. Knit 3 rows with main yarn. Transfer stitches for 2 by 2 rib. Hang comb and weights. Tension 4/4. Knit 16 rows. Transfer to main bed. Pick up the heels of those stitches of the last stocking stitch row which are at the bottom of the columns of knit stitches and place on main bed needles.

Pairs of heels being placed on the same needles as the columns of knit stitches

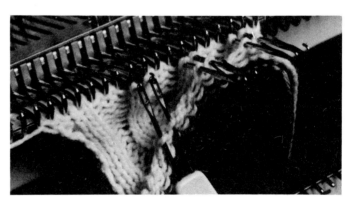

Tension 6; knit 3 rows. Pick up all the loops of first row of stocking stitch knitted in main yarn and place on needles. Tension 8; knit 1 row. Break off yarn, leaving long end. Tension 6. Release on waste knitting.

Pocket Lining Arrange 18 needles for 2 by 2 rib. Cast on. Knit selvedge. Tension 4../4.. (main tension for garment). Knit 30 rows. Transfer to main bed. Release on waste knitting.

NOTE The lining could be released on ribbed waste knitting, but it is very much easier to put back on the machine if this method is followed.

Pocket heading released from the machine, right side facing

Part of Left Front   Arrange 46 needles for 2 × 2 rib. Cast on. Knit selvedge. Tension 4/4; knit 24 rows. Tension 4../4..; knit 30 rows. Now we decide where to place the pocket. Following the suggested method, we have:

Front − Pocket = 46 − 18 = 28

A quarter of 28 is 7, so the pocket will be placed approximately 7 stitches from the side seam, which will be at the left of our practice piece. The exact number depends on matching up the rib formation. The knit stitches of the heading must lie on top of knit stitches on the garment, and these are on the main bed in this case. We can therefore place the pocket starting either on stitch 5 or stitch 9 counting from the left. Stitch 7, which we calculated as the position will not do because it is on the rib bed. Stitch 5 is too near the side seam, so we will position the pocket starting on stitch 9, marked x in the diagram. The right end of the pocket position is marked y.

Small size front

```
               x                                    y
MB   l l o o l l o o l l o o l l o o l l o o l l o o l l o o l l o o l l o o l l o o l l
RB     o o l l o o l l o o l l o o l l o o l l o o l l o o l l o o l l o o l l o o l l o o
```

Transfer stitches so that the 18 stitches from x to y are on the rib bed. Lower the rib bed one position and place the stitches of the pocket heading on the same needles. The right side of the front is facing away from you, so the right side of the heading must be towards you, that is 'right sides together'. Make sure you get it right: the purl side of the waste knitting must face you. Notice the position of the heading in the diagram. There are 2 rib bed stitches on both sides of the 18 heading stitches, like this:

```
MB   l l o o l l o o o o o o o o o o o o o o o o o o o o l l o o l l o o l l o o l l o o l l
                      l l l l l l l l l l l l l l l l l l   Stitches of pocket heading on rib bed needles
RB     o o l l o o l l l l l l l l l l l l l l l l l l l l l l o o l l o o l l o o l l o o l l o o
```

74

Stitches of pocket heading are being placed on the same needles as the 18 pocket opening stitches on the rib bed

When all the stitches are in position cast off using length of yarn left on the heading.

The next stage is to place loops of the first row of waste knitting on the lining onto empty main bed needles, making sure that the lining faces the way it did when it was knitted. It is easier to put the stitches back from stocking stitch than from rib. Transfer for rib.

Pocket lining in position on main bed needles ready to be transferred for rib

Pin the pocket lining to the front with a knitting needle and hang a claw weight on it. Put side weights on wire hangers over the ends of pocket. Then, if knitting a real garment, complete the front.

In the practice piece knit 30 rows. Cast off. Sew sides of pocket lining to wrong side of garment piece, and bottom of lining to last row of welt. Sew edges of heading to the garment.

PRACTISING BUTTONHOLES

Although some of the buttonholes described do not belong to the cardigan in this chapter, it is helpful at this stage in the ribbing course to make a sample for future reference.

Please do not be tempted to skip this bit, thinking you will come back to it later. Many knitters groan about buttonholes, and they are quite easy really! Some of the buttonholes are made by methods which are a little different from the ones usually described. The aim is to make a buttonhole which is really neat without the need for sewing round it afterwards.

Knitted in 1 × 1 Rib   Refer to Chapter 2 if necessary.

1. 1-stitch Buttonhole

Cast on 13 stitches. Central stitch is on main bed. This is the centre of the buttonhole. To weight work use a wire weight hanger, holding it down by hand until selvedge has been knitted, then hanging small weight. Tension 3/3 (as welt). Knit 10 rows.

Transfer centre stitch 'a' on main bed to a working needle next to it on rib bed. Leave main bed needle in working position.

```
                            a
    MB      l o l o l o l o l o l o l
                           ↙
    RB      l o l o l o l o l o l
```

Stitch from 4th needle on left of main bed has been transferred to 3rd needle on left of rib bed

Knit 1 row, and stop and look. You now have a cast on loop on the empty needle, and a buttonhole beneath it where the stitch was transferred. This very small buttonhole is suitable only for baby clothes. Knit 10 rows to the next buttonhole.

2. 2-stitch Buttonhole

This is made by transferring stitch 'a' to the rib bed and stitch 'b' to the main bed, leaving needles in working position.

76

```
           a
MB   | o | o | o | o | o | o |
                ↙   ↗
RB     | o | o | o | o | o |
                b
```

Stitch from 4th needle on right of main bed has been transferred to needle 10 on rib bed. Stitch from 3rd needle on right of rib bed has been transferred to 3rd needle of right of main bed

When the next row is knitted the two empty needles will cast on. Knit a few more rows and cast off.

Knitted in 2 × 2 rib (2 up 2 down)   Refer to Chapter 5 if necessary.

2-stitch Buttonhole

Cast on 14 stitches. The wrong side of the knitting is facing the knitter. Tension 4/4; knit 10 rows. A 1-stitch buttonhole is not suitable for this rib.

```
MB   | | o o | | o o | | o o | |
              ↖   ↗
RB   o o | | o o | | o o | | o o
              a b
```

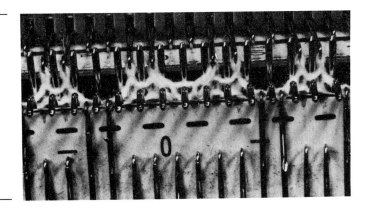

Stitches 'a b' transferred to nearest main bed needles

MB | | o o | 2 * o 2 | o o | |
RB   o o | | o o o * o o | | o o

*Needles marked * put in working position and 1 row knitted giving following arrangement:*

               * †
MB | | o o | | | o | | | o o | |
RB   o o | | | o o o | o o | | o o
             † *

*Main bed stitch marked * transferred to right and rib bed stitch marked * transferred to left both on same bed and 1 row knitted. This tightens the loops and makes a neater hole. Before continuing extra main bed stitch is transferred to rib bed to make rib formation right*

The finished buttonhole removed from machine

NOTE: In some sizes in cardigan pattern alternate buttonholes are made by transferring *main* bed stitches. When doing this turn diagrams upside down to see how to make transfers.

Knitted in 2 × 2 rib (2 up 1 down)   Refer to Chapter 7 if necessary. Use fine yarn and knit over the width of 17 main bed needles. Tension 1./1..

```
MB      | | o | | o | | o | | o | | o | |
                          ↖ ↗
RB      o | | o | | o | | o | | o | | o
                          a b
```

Stitches 'a b' transferred to the main bed

```
MB      | | o | | o | 2 o 2 | o | | o | |
RB      o | | o | | o o * o | | o | | o
```

*Rib bed needle marked * left in working position and 1 row knitted*

79

```
MB   | | o | | o | | * | | o | | o | |
RB     o | | o | | o | o o | | o | | o
```

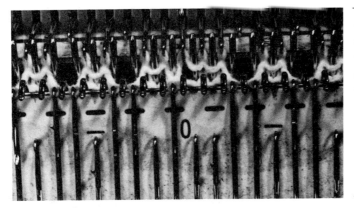

*Main bed needle marked * pushed to working position. Stitch made on rib bed in previous row transferred to left and 1 row knitted*

```
MB   | | o | | o | | o | | o | | o | |
RB     o | | o | | o | | o | | o | | o
```

Stitch made on main bed in previous row transferred to rib bed to make rib formation correct. Buttonhole complete. Knitting continues

Knit about 10 rows, make another buttonhole, knit a few more rows. Cast off.

The 2-stitch buttonholes you have knitted will take half-inch buttons. If you wish to use larger buttons in either form of 2 by 2 rib, you will need a vertical buttonhole 5, 7 or 9 rows long. There are ways of making larger horizontal buttonholes, and a method is given in Chapter 12.

Vertical Buttonhole

Practise this in both forms of 2 by 2 ribbing. Cast on and knit to first buttonhole position. Carriage right. The buttonhole will be made between two main bed needles, and must be positioned a suitable distance from the edge, depending on yarn and type of garment. Set both carriages to hold. Push all needles to left of buttonhole to holding position.

```
       †..........................................†       †...† Needles to holding position
MB     | | o | | o | | o | | o |c| o | | o | |     c = centre. This is buttonhole
RB       o | | o | | o | | o | | o | | o | | o     position
       †................................†
```

Stitches in holding position ready for knitting buttonhole. 7 rows knitted on stitches at the right. Carriage left

Knit required number of rows on stitches at right. This will always be an uneven number of rows finishing carriage left.

```
                              2
MB     | | o | | o | | o | | o |c| o | | o | |
RB       o | | o | | o | | o | | o | | o | | o
                                      1
```

The yarn is hooked in the needle marked 1

Carriages are set to slip and moved back to right. In this row nothing is knitted. Release the holding cams, leaving carriages still set to slip, and knit to left. Needles at right will not knit, those at left will.

Change position of hooked yarn (not the stitch under it) to needle marked 2. Push needles at right to holding position and set holding cams again.

* Knit 2 rows. Pick up thread which crosses centre. Put it on needle 2. *

This is the thread to pick up

Repeat from * to * twice more. The buttonhole is complete with no ends to sew in, so go on knitting to the next one.

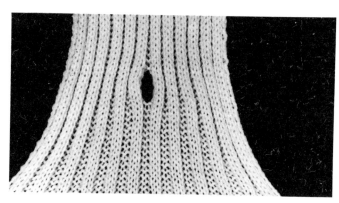

The finished buttonhole

RIBBED BUTTON AND BUTTONHOLE BANDS – METHODS OF KNITTING AND ATTACHING

To Knit a Vertical Ribbed Band
Suitable for:

1. Single bed garment
2. Garment knitted in different rib from welt

Unsuitable for attaching to a garment knitted in same rib as welt because tension of band and tension of main fabric will be different.

Tension and needle arrangement: As welt.

To Calculate: The only satisfactory way is to measure length required and to work out number of rows from tension swatch of rib to be used.

Bands for Round Neck Cardigans

1. Bands finishing right at neck are attached after neckband has been knitted and attached.
2. Bands finishing below neckband are attached before neckband is knitted.

    In both cases calculate length required, then work out position of button-holes allowing for buttonhole in neckband in example 2. Allow 1.5 cm (⅝ inch) below bottom buttonhole and above top one. It is possible to make a very small adjustment to the number of rows to be knitted in order to space buttonholes evenly. Button band is the same length, and it is usually better to knit it first as a check on the calculations.

    Either of these bands are best started as extra stitches at centre edge of front welt. The extra stitches are threaded onto stitch holder or length of waste yarn on completion of welt and the bands knitted up and attached afterwards.

Band for a Vee-necked Cardigan

This is knitted in a continuous piece. Measure right round opening. Calculate approximately how many rows are needed. Measure and calculate accurately buttonhole section including position of buttonholes.

Knit beginning of band as extra stitches at centre of front welt on buttonhole side, remembering that at least one buttonhole will be made during knitting of welt. This must be accounted for in calculating the spacing of the buttonholes.

DO remember the buttonhole in the welt. It is devastating to knit to the end of the front, and find it missing!

Do not put extra stitches on welt of button front. The extended buttonhole piece goes right to the bottom on the button side.

When back and both fronts are complete, seam shoulders. Return stitches for band to needles. When full length has been knitted release work on waste knitting. Attach band to garment. Any surplus can be unravelled or more can be knitted if required before binding off.

Either of these bands would be suitable if you decided to convert the pullovers in Chapters 5 and 7 to cardigans.

To Knit Ribbed Bands Sideways
Suitable for most cardigans and used in the pattern in this chapter.

Tension: As welt

To Calculate: In a round-necked cardigan this type of band extends the full length of the front, and is attached after the neckband has been knitted and joined on. Measure length required and work out number of stitches and spacing of buttonholes from tension swatch.

In a Vee-neck cardigan bands should join at centre back if possible. If necessary a separate piece can be knitted for the back neck with joins on the shoulder seams or back raglan seams. If fine yarn is being used for a Vee-neck cardigan there may not be enough needles to produce a wide enough piece of knitting for the fronts. In that case it is better to knit a different type of band. This can either be a vertical ribbed band, or a vertical circular knitted band. The method for the latter is described in Chapter 10.

ADAPTING THE JUMPER PATTERN FOR A CARDIGAN
It is not a difficult project to adapt any jumper pattern, providing it is taken step by step. The back and sleeves are exactly the same, so start with those, turning back to Chapter 6 for the instructions to serve as a reminder of 2 by 2 rib before you knit the fronts with their pockets and bands and buttonholes.

TO KNIT THE CARDIGAN: ROUND NECK: RAGLAN SLEEVES: 2 × 2 RIB THROUGHOUT (See Pages 3, 7 and 8.)

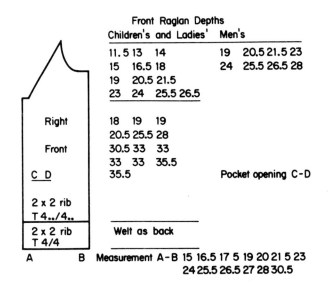

	Front Raglan Depths	
	Children's and Ladies'	Men's
	11.5 13 14	19 20.5 21.5 23
	15 16.5 18	24 25.5 26.5 28
	19 20.5 21.5	
	23 24 25.5 26.5	
Right	18 19 19	
	20.5 25.5 28	
Front	30.5 33 33	
	33 33 35.5	
C D	35.5	Pocket opening C-D
2 x 2 rib		
T 4../4..		
2 x 2 rib	Welt as back	
T 4/4		
A B	Measurement A-B 15 16.5 17 5 19 20 21 5 23	
	24 25.5 26.5 27 28 30.5	

Tension swatches as in Chapter 6:

For welts and bands	Tension 4/4	34 stitches and 44 rows = 10 cm (4 inches)
For main knitting	Tension 4../4..	30 stitches and 40 rows = 10 cm (4 inches)

```
         s
MB    |  |  o  o  |  |  o  o  |  |  o  o  |  |
RB    o  o  |  |  o  o  |  |  o  o  |  |  o  o
```

s = seaming stitch.

This is the setting for back and sleeves. For fronts, pocket headings and linings, front bands, and neckband, end needles are sometimes differently arranged, as is explained in the pattern.

Wrong side is facing knitter.

To Fit Bust Sizes	Centimetres	56	61	66	71	76	81	86	91	97	102	107	112	117
	Inches	22	24	26	28	30	32	34	36	38	40	42	44	46

Back and Sleeves

Knit as given for the jumper, Chapter 6 Pages **52** to **55**.

Fronts

First knit pocket headings and linings.

Pocket Headings Knit 2 as in practice piece. Cast on and knit several rows with waste yarn at Tension 6 on following number of stitches

22	22	22	26	26	26	30	30	30	30	34	34	38

Knit 1 row with nylon cord, 3 rows with main yarn. Transfer for rib. Hang comb and weights. RC 000. Tension 4/4. Knit to RC

16	16	16	20	20	20	20	20	20	24	24	24	24

Transfer to main bed. Pick up loops below knit columns. Tension 6. Knit 3 rows. Pick up loops from 1st row of main yarn. Tension 8. Knit 1 row. Tension 6. Release on waste knitting.

Pocket Linings Knit 2 as in practice piece on same number of needles as pocket headings. Cast on. Knit selvedge. RC 000. Tension 4../4... Knit to RC

30	32	34	34	36	36	40	40	40	40	40	40	40

then release on waste knitting

Next calculate stitches for front, and decide on needle arrangement. Halve stitches of jumper front, adding 2 stitches to sizes 7–13 so that the total is divisible by 4 plus 1 stitch. Since the raglan must be the same as on the back these 2 stitches have been added to the first group on the neck to be put into holding position. The odd stitch will be on main bed at centre for joining to front band. Needle arrangement for left front will be

```
            s                 s
MB    |  |  o  o  |  |  o  o  |
RB    o  o  |  |  o  o  |  |  o
```

The left side of the diagram is the underarm edge which joins up with back. On the right front there will be 1 main bed stitch at left and 2 at right.

Left Front Wrong side facing knitter.

All Sizes Arrange needles for 2 × 2 rib. Cast on

45	49	53	57	61	65	69	73	77	81	85	89	93

Knit welt. RC 000. Tension 4../4... Knit to RC

30	32	34	34	36	36	40	40	40	40	40	40	40

Insert pocket and heading as in practice piece. Pocket position starts on following stitch from left

9	9	9	9	13	13	13	13	13	17	17	21	21

Knit to RC

72	76	76	82	102	112	122	132	132	132	132	142	142

Men's Adjust length to match back.

Armhole and Raglan Raglan on left, neck on right. RC 000. Knit 1 row. At beginning of next row cast off following stitches:

Children's and Ladies'

5	6	6	7	7	7	6	8	8	9	9	10	11

Men's

					7	7	7	8	8	8	9	9

Work all decreasings by fully-fashioned method.

Children's and Ladies' Decrease 1 stitch at left on next row and every following alternate row. Knit to RC (carriage left)

31	35	39	43	49	51	59	63	69	73	79	83	89

Number of stitches

26	27	29	30	31	34	35	35	36	37	38	39	39

Men's Decrease 1 stitch at left on next and every following 3rd row. Number of decreasings

					6	6	4	4	4	2	4	–

Number of stitches

					52	56	62	65	69	75	76	–

Knit 2 rows. RC

					20	20	14	14	14	8	14	–

Decrease 1 stitch at left on next and every following alternate row to RC (carriage left)

					57	61	67	71	77	81	87	91

Number of stitches

					34	36	36	37	38	39	40	40

Shape Neck at right using holding position as in jumper, transferring stitches to main bed when they are put

to holding position.
All Sizes Put stitches to holding
position at right

5	6	6	7	8	8	9	9	10	11	12	13	13

Shape neck by putting stitches at right
into holding position on alternate rows
always when carriage is at left. Wrap
inside needles.

Children's and Ladies' Stitches to
holding position on alternate rows

4 stitches all sizes

then

2	2	2	2	2	Sizes 6–13: 2 stitches 4 times

then 1 stitch every row following
number of times

5	5	6	6	6	Sizes 6–13: 3

AT SAME TIME decrease 1 stitch at
raglan edge on alternate rows always
when carriage is at right following
number of times

8	8	9	9	9	Sizes 6–13: 9

Put remaining 2 stitches to holding
position. RC

46	50	56	60	66	68	76	80	86	90	96	100	106

Total stitches in holding position front
neck

18	19	20	21	22	25	26	26	27	28	29	30	30

Men's Stitches to holding position
alternate rows

Sizes 6–13: 4 stitches once

then

2 stitches 3 times

then 1 stitch every row

5 times

AT SAME TIME decrease 1 stitch at
raglan edge on alternate rows always
when carriage is at right following
number of times

Sizes 6–13: 10

Put remaining 2 stitches to holding
position. RC

76	80	86	90	96	100	106	110

Total stitches in holding position front
neck

25	26	26	27	28	29	30	30

All Sizes Release neck stitches on
waste-knitting.

Right Front Knit as left front reversing
end stitch arrangement. Position pocket
counting stitches from right. Reverse
shapings of neck and raglan. Before
knitting neckband join all raglan seams.

Neckband This is knitted and attached
as for jumper, Pages **55** to **57**, adding 4
stitches to sizes 7–13.

Button Band
Arrange following needles for rib
NOTE : end needle arrangement:
Sizes 1, 3, 4, 5, 7–13 where stitches
are divisible by 4

100	106	112	120	136	146	156	172	172	184	184	196	196

```
MB    l o o l l o o l l .... o o l
RB    o l l o o l l o o .... l l o
```

Sizes 2 and 6 where stitches are divisible
by 2 but not 4

```
MB    l o o l l o o l l .... o o l l l
RB    o l l o o l l o o .... l l o o o
```

Stitches underlined are first button
position, (or buttonhole).
NOTE : This arrangement means that
last stitch will always be on main bed.
Cast on. Tension 4/4. RC 000. Knit to
RC
Transfer to main bed. Tension 6. Knit
1 row. Attach front to band, wrong side
facing, as follows:
1. Ladies' cardigans Left front, welt at
right. Right front, welt at left
2. Men's cardigans Reverse of
Ladies'
Tension 10. Knit 1 row. Cast off.

Buttonhole Bands
Knit on same number of needles.
In sizes 2, 6 where end needle
arrangements on button band are not
identical, reverse ends. Knit half
required number of rows, then make
buttonholes positioned as given below.
Buttonholes are 2 stitches wide. There
are 7 stitches at both ends. Number of
stitches between buttonholes
Number of buttonholes
NOTE : Button and buttonhole bands
have been calculated for lengths of
garments given in pattern. If any
adjustment to length is made, bands
must also be adjusted. (Information
follows.)

Knit to RC	8	8	8	10	10	10	10	10	12	12	12	12	12
Number of stitches between buttonholes	26	28	22	24	28	24	26	24	24	26	26	28	28
Number of buttonholes	4	4	5	5	5	6	6	7	7	7	7	7	7

To Make Up   Finish off pockets by sewing linings to inside of fronts, taking care not to show stitches through to right side. Sew edges of headings to fronts keeping sequence of rib. Sew underarm and sleeve seams. Sew on buttons.

FOR FUTURE REFERENCE – CALCULATING THE POSITION OF BUTTONHOLES

1. Work out the following:

Approximate stitches for band
Stitches for each buttonhole
Stitches at each end

2. Put pins in front of garment to find out how many buttonholes will look right.

Remember that too few cause gaps, and too many are a nuisance.

3. From this work out band as follows in relation to size 76. By measurement let us suppose we have decided we need 138 stitches for the band. The buttonholes will be 2 stitches wide and we need 5. There will be 7 stitches at each end.

4. *To Calculate:*

$$5 \text{ buttons} \times 2 \text{ stitches} = 10$$
$$2 \text{ ends} \times 7 \text{ stitches} = 14$$

that is, 24 used out of 138, leaving 114 stitches to be divided into the 4 spaces between the buttonholes.

114 divided by 4 is 28 with 2 stitches to spare. We cannot do with spare stitches, so instead of starting with 138 stitches we will cast on 136 arranged as follows:

```
MB    l o o l l o o l l o o .... o o l
RB    o l l o o l l o o l l .... l l o
```

If you find the arithmetic of knitting a chore, try sitting at your machine working out all these various arrangements with the empty needles. A bit like using a counting frame! It is not important how we arrive at an answer, as long as we understand what the aim is and get there one way or another!

TO RECAP
In this chapter you have learnt:
  how to make a variety of buttonholes
  how to insert pockets in a ribbed garment
  where to position pockets
  about ribbed front bands in general
  about sideways knitted bands in detail
  how to work out buttonhole positions in sideways bands
  how to adapt a jumper pattern to make a cardigan...and...
you have been given a cardigan pattern in 2 by 2 rib in thirteen sizes.

9

CIRCULAR KNITTING: A COLLECTION OF ITEMS

So far we have only knitted a few rows of circular knitting when casting on for ribs. Now we come to consider whole garments and articles knitted this way. There are two ways of casting on: closed end, which we shall use for a hot water bottle cover and a scarf; and open end, which we shall use for a small child's jumper. (See Pages 1 and 3.)

TO MAKE A CLOSED-END CAST ON IN CIRCULAR KNITTING

1. Half pitch: both carriages set to knit.
2. Select 60 needles on both beds arranged like this:

```
MB    | | | | | | | | | | | | | |
RB     | | | | | | | | | | | | | | |
```

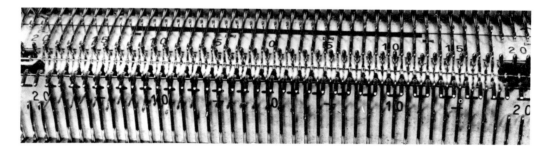

Closed-end cast on for circular knitting

Notice that we have broken the needle rule at the right. If we wish to knit a flat piece of circular knitting we must have an equal number of stitches on both beds.

3. Align needles.
4. Thread waste yarn.
5. Zig zag row. Tension 0/0.
6. Insert comb taking care that the yarn end at the right, which is not in the place you have been used to, is secured, otherwise the right hand rib bed needle will not knit.
7. Set carriages for circular knitting:

> Main carriage to knit to right, slip to left
> Rib carriage to knit to left, slip to right

Tension 2/2; knit 2 rows. Set beds to full pitch. Stitches are now arranged like this:

```
MB   | | | | | | | | | | | | | |
RB   | | | | | | | | | | | | | |
```

Correct setting for long piece of circular knitting; beds set to full pitch

It is incorrect to use half pitch position for circular knitting. It makes the ends stretch.
8. Tension 4/4; knit 2 rows. RC 000. Tension 6/6. Main yarn. Knit 60 rows, marking 21st stitches on main bed.

Carriage is at left. Change to waste yarn. Knit 12 rows. Release from machine.
9. Block out tension piece and press lightly. The measurements of the swatch used for the scarf were:

> 30 stitches (main bed only counted) and 80 rows = 10 cm

NOTE Twice as many rows as required for 10 cm stocking stitch. Since this is

91

the same yarn as the stocking stitch jumper in Chapter 5, that tension swatch could have been used by doubling the number of rows.

However, it is possible that the tensions of the two beds are not the same. In that case the instruction book will tell you what difference you should make between the tensions of the two beds. Even so, you may need to experiment a little with tension swatches until both sides match. Get your main bed right by knitting on it at stocking stitch tension for the type of yarn in use, then adjust the rib bed tension until both halves are the same.

When you have knitted about 400 rows you will need to re-hang the comb. If you are using a comb with bar the method is the same as that given on Page 27.

With an ordinary comb there is a difference. It is not possible to push the teeth through between the beds when you are doing circular knitting, so it is necessary to improvise. Without removing the wire, roll the knitting round the comb until it is just below the machine. Pin through the folds using a knitting needle and re-hang the weights. They will have to hang outside the knitting, and two large ones should be sufficient.

TO KNIT THE SCARF

The scarf will be knitted in one colour only, with contrast colour fringe. There are complications when knitting circular stripes, and they are best left to the second Ribber Course Book.

Arrange 68 needles on both beds for circular knitting. The width of the scarf will be approximately 22.5 cm (9 inches). Adjust this if you wish.

Using main yarn cast on and knit 5 rows as at beginning of tension piece. Full pitch. RC 000. Tension 6/6. Knit to RC 800 (1 metre) or required length. Tension 8/8. Knit 2 rows.

To cast off transfer rib bed stitches to main bed letting main bed stitches drop behind the latches, and making sure rib bed ones stay in the hooks. When you have finished transferring stitches straighten up the needle butts using the straight edge of the needle pusher. Check that all stitches are in the right position. Gently push the needles back so that the main bed stitches are knitted off over the rib bed ones leaving only 1 stitch on each needle. Break off yarn leaving long end. Knit 6 rows in waste yarn. Release from the machine.

Fold back waste knitting. Using end of main yarn backstitch through loops of the last row of main colour. Fasten off and unravel waste.

Fringe Wind contrast yarn round a book about 12 cm wide (4¾ inches). Wind and cut about 50 lengths of yarn to start with. Arrange it in bunches of 3–6 pieces, depending upon thickness, and, using the latch tool pull a double loop through the scarf about 1 cm (⅜ inch) from the edge, and knot it. You will soon discover what looks right. If the bunches are too close to each other they will stretch the edge.

TO KNIT A HOT WATER BOTTLE COVER

There are several points to note. We shall be doing circular knitting with ladders so the heat comes out, but we do not want ladders in the casting on because they would make a weak edge. Secondly we need to make holes through which to thread a cord, and, lastly, we must cast off each bed separately.

Arrange 63 needles on both beds as shown on Page 90. Cast on and knit first 5 rows exactly as before.

Full pitch. Arrange stitches as shown below, transferring those not required sideways on same bed, not across beds. RC 000.

```
MB   | | | | | | | o | | | | | | | o | | | | | | |
RB   | | | | | | | o | | | | | | | o | | | | | | |
```

Tension 6/6. Knit 280 rows.

Make a row of holes on both beds by transferring the middle stitch of each group of 7 to the neighbouring needle, leaving empty needles in working position.

It looks better if we always transfer stitches in the same direction. This means working towards the left on one bed and the right on the other: a small point, but it makes a difference to the appearance.

Bring ladder needles into working position. Knit 20 rows.

Tension 10/8. Knit 2 rows.

Tension 6/6. Using waste yarn knit 12 rows. Release from machine.

Turn work purl side outside. Stretch over finger, and using latch tool crochet each stitch of large tension row through the next stitch in exactly the same way as you would if it were on the machine. Finally pull the thread through the last loop and fasten off. The casting off can be done on the machine, but is easier in circular knitting when hand-held. Unravel waste.

Cord

Cords can be flat, in which case there are the same number of stitches on both beds, or round, when one more stitch is needed on the main bed.

Arrange needles as shown here:

```
MB    | | | |
RB     | | |
```

Knit zig zag row. Hang wire weight hanger and small weight. Knit first 5 rows as before. RC 000. Knit 300 rows. Break off yarn. Thread end through all loops, pull up and fasten off.

Fasten off all ends. Make crochet edging at top if desired. Thread cord as shown in diagram. Join ends together.

Threading cord which goes twice round
top of hot water bottle

TO MAKE AN OPEN-END CAST ON IN CIRCULAR KNITTING

Sometimes we need open stocking stitch loops at the beginning of circular knitting, and sometimes we need ribbing. In the child's jumper both are required: ribbing for circular back and front, and stocking stitch loops at the bottom of the sleeves to gather into the ribbed wrist band, which is knitted and attached afterwards.

There are two ways of starting open-ended circular knitting, depending on what is to follow it.

When open-ended stocking stitch loops are needed, start with a closed circular cast on using waste yarn. Knit about 16 rows; that is, 8 on each bed. When the work is finished and the comb removed just cut along the zig zag to open up the circle.

When starting with rib for a circular garment which is less than 200 stitches all round, the rib is knitted for both back and front in one piece. When it is complete all the stitches are transferred to the main bed, and 2 stocking stitch rows knitted. It is easier to replace stocking stitch on the needles than it is to replace ribbing. Half of the ribbing at the same end as the point of the comb wire is removed on waste knitting. The wire is pulled out under that half only, releasing the selvedge so that the ribbing can be turned round to face the stitches which are still on the main bed needles. The stitches of the released half are put on the rib bed needles so that a circle is formed. If the ribbing has an odd number of stitches it will be necessary to increase on one of the beds to make the numbers even.

If the back or front of the garment is more than 100 needles in width, two pieces of ribbing are knitted. The first is removed from the machine after knitting 2 rows stocking stitch. When the stitches of the second piece have been transferred to the main bed and 2 rows of stocking stitch have been knitted, the first piece is put onto the rib bed needles opposite the second, with purl stitches facing each other.

In both cases only half the ribbing is attached to comb and weights. Pin the other side to it using a knitting needle, then the weights will be effective for all the work.

Starting with a hem instead of ribbing is also possible, but as it is not needed for this jumper it will be left for Book 2, unless, that is, you care to puzzle it out for yourself!

TO KNIT CHILD'S JUMPER

To Fit Chest Sizes	Centimetres	41	46	51	56
	Inches	16	18	20	22

94

1 x 1 rib — 2.5
Back and Front — 24, 26.5, 28.5, 31
25.5 28 30.5 33 — 4

10.5 11
12 12.5
Sleeve 2 alike — 14, 16, 18, 20
4

NOTE : Width of jumper and sleeve is measured as seen, in a circle. The hemline is double the measurement given on the block. Tension : circular knitting.

30 stitches on both beds (60) and 80 rows = 10 cm

Back and Front Knit 1 circular piece after folding welt.
Arrange needles on both beds for 1 × 1 rib as follows — 151 167 181 197
Cast on and knit selvedge. RC 000. Tension 4/4. Knit to RC — 16 16 16 16
Halve the work as described and turn into circle. Increase 1 stitch so that there are the following stitches on both beds arranged ready for circular knitting — 76 84 92 99
Tension 6/6. Set machine for circular knitting. RC 000. Knit to RC — 110 120 130 140
The knitting now continues separately for back and front. Set main bed to slip. Knit 6 rows in waste yarn on rib bed. Release stitches from machine. Continue with machine set up as ribber. This means leaving comb and weights in position, rib bed raised, ribber arm connected. * Main bed to knit. RC 000. Knit to RC — 42 46 50 54
Transfer stitches for 1 × 1 rib. Tension 4/4. RC 000. * Knit to RC — 10 All sizes
Tension 10/8. Knit 1 row. Remove comb and cast off with latch tool. Turn work round. Put second side on main bed needles. This time it is easier to work on the main bed as a single bed until you knit the rib so change the sinker plate and keep the rib bed down. Repeat from * to *. When you have transferred for rib insert comb and wire by gently pushing teeth up between stitches taking care not to split yarn. Knit rib as before.

Sleeves Knit 2 alike.
Cast on for circular knitting using waste yarn on following needles on both beds — 32 34 36 38
Knit approximately 16 rows. Carriage right. RC 000. Main yarn. Knit to RC — 112 128 144 160
Tension 10/8. Knit 2 rows. Cast off open-ended (as hot water bottle cover).
Cut through the zig zag to open up the circle.

Welts
Arrange needles for 1 × 1 rib as follows — 33 35 37 39
Cast on and knit 16 rows as before. Knit 2 rows at Tension 5/5.
Transfer all stitches to main bed. Carriage right.

To Join Welt to Sleeve This must be done half at a time since sleeves are circular. With knit side of sleeve towards rib place loops of first row of sleeve on welt needles, 2 stitches to a needle except at ends. Set machine to slip. Push needles containing rib and sleeve stitches to upper working or holding position. Tension 10. With machine set to knit stitches back (that is with holding cam released), knit 1 row. First purl of row will knit, rest will slip.

Cast off joined up end using latch tool. Put last loop on needle next in knitting, and leave it in working position. Move carriage back to right. Place rest of sleeve on needles in same way. Knit a Tension 10 row on all needles except the one at the right which has already been knitted. Starting with that needle complete casting off.

To Make Up Seam welts. Seam ribs together for about 2 cm (¾ inch) at armhole ends of neck ribs. Sew sleeves into armholes. Make loops on front shoulders and sew on buttons to match on back.

ABOUT THE JUMPER PATTERN

The two larger sizes were adapted from the pattern given in Chapter 5. The difference between the two patterns is that in Chapter 5 there is a square armhole and in this chapter the armhole is not cast off at all, and therefore the sleeves are shorter. All the other sizes in the Chapter 5 pattern can be knitted in this way. Remember to start all the welts with an uneven number of stitches if you are knitting 1 by 1 ribbing, to make them divisible by 4 plus 2 extra stitches if you are knitting 2 by 2 ribbing (2 up 2 down), and divisible by 3 plus 2 if you are knitting the other form of 2 by 2 ribbing (2 up 1 down).

TO RECAP

In this chapter you have learnt:

> *how to make a closed-end cast on for circular knitting*
> *how to make an open-end cast on for circular knitting*
> *two more ways of binding off a piece of work...and...*

you have been given several quick-to-knit patterns suitable for presents.

10

FULL NEEDLE RIB AND TWO VARIATIONS; TEE SHIRT

In this chapter we are going to knit another kind of 1 × 1 ribbing. It has various names – Full Needle rib, Close rib, Double rib, and Every Needle rib being the four most often used in connection with the Japanese machines. In this book we will refer to Full Needle rib. We are going to use it to knit a tee shirt, and we shall also knit two variations, called long stitch and pin tucks or ridge stitch. One of these may be used for the collar and the pocket.

Full Needle rib uses all needles on both beds, which means that there are no needles within the width of the knitting in non-working position. Therefore the rib bed is set to half pitch as we did for the zig zag for circular knitting, only this time we keep to the needle rule with both end stitches on the main bed. Because there are so many needles in use it is better, when you are not used to knitting this stitch, to use 2 or 3 ply – nothing thicker. We shall use 2 ply for the tee shirt.

It is possible to substitute two strands of industrial yarn (2/30s) for 2 ply. Use two cones if you can, because small amounts wound off can cause trouble for inexperienced knitters with such a lightweight yarn. Thread both ends together through the yarn mast. Do not allow the cones to touch each other, and keep any other yarns which are threaded up well away from your fine yarns. There is a tendency for the fine yarn to attract other yarns and draw them up through the yarn mast, and that is not helpful!

If you are a beginner, avoid knitting in 2/30s until you have had a little more experience unless you are unable to obtain 2 ply yarn.

Sometimes when using this very fine yarn two-stranded (two ends knitted together), one of the ends misses the needles on one bed in some of the stitches. Fortunately, if this is going to happen, it usually happens right at the start in the zig zag row.

97

There are several possible causes. The first check should be on the cones. If they are touching each other, or touching anything else, put that right and try again. Failing that, check on the threading through the yarn mast. Sometimes one strand gets wound round one of the bits twice. If it still will not knit after all that, then you must check the set of the ribber to the main bed and the alignment of the needles. Put the beds back to full pitch. Then loosen the two screws which hold the ribber to the main bed. Loosen, but do not remove, the small clamps. Put one hand under the centre of the rib bed, and pull it slightly towards you and up. This action takes the ribber bracket further inside the main bed. Tighten the screws, and the clamps. Then make certain the needles are really opposite. When all that has been done you should achieve a perfect zig zag.

CASTING ON AND KNITTING TENSION SWATCH

1. Half pitch
2. Select 60 needles on the main bed, and arrange rib bed needles as below:

```
MB    | | | | | | | | | | | |    Main Tension 2/2
RB      | | | | | | | | | | | |
```

There are two differences to note when knitting the many stitches which can be knitted using this needle arrangement. They are as follows:

a) When counting stitches in this rib only the main bed needles in work are counted. In a pattern we shall, in this book, say 'over the width of 60 main bed needles arrange needles of both beds for full needle rib'.

Not all patterns make this point absolutely clear. If you are at all uncertain check by working out the stitches for the required measurement from the given tension swatch measurements.

b) In Jones + Brother and Knitmaster machines there is an accessory in the ribber equipment which is called either the 'fine knit bar' or the 'close knit bar'. This must be put into position behind the main bed gate pegs whenever full needle rib setting is used. Its purpose is to prevent the main bed needles bending down as low as they usually do when the stitches are knitted. This helps stitches to drop right off closed latches when the next row is knitted.

If you put the close knit bar in position along half of the needle bed and put some needles into holding position in both halves, and then press down on their stems you will feel the difference and understand what I mean. The close knit bar prevents some of the downward movement of the needles, helping the stitches to knit off properly. If you forget to put it in place, after a few rows you will find stitches on top of closed latches.

3. Align needles.
4. Thread yarn.
5. Use waste yarn (2 ply).

It is very important to use the same weight waste yarn always. If you use thicker waste yarn the edge of the knitting will be distorted.

   Tension 0/0. Knit zig zag row.
6. Hang comb.

Take care how you push it through; the threads are very close to each other.

7. Knit selvedge, exactly as you have done in the previous chapters, then hang weights.
8. Tension 2/2. Set both carriages to knit. Knit 10 rows in waste yarn. Change to main yarn. RC 000. Knit 30 rows. Mark the 21st main bed stitch both sides of centre. Knit 30 rows. Change to waste yarn. Knit 10 rows. Cast off. There are three methods. Try them in turn on your practice pieces, and use the one you like best when you knit a garment:

   a) Transfer all rib bed stitches to main bed. Lower rib bed and cover it. Knit end 2 stitches together as if decreasing. Cast off by transferring stitch to next needle behind gate pegs; normal single bed method.
   b) As 1, but knit a row at Tension 10 and cast off using the latch tool. This gives a purl row before the cast off edge.
   c) Do not transfer stitches. Tension 7/7. Knit 1 row. Use the latch tool to cast off, taking stitches from the two beds alternately. This is casting off in rib, and gives greater elasticity to the edge than the other methods.

9. Block out and rest fabric. Measure as before.
   The measurements of swatch used for garment shown on Pages 4, 7 and 8 were:

   32 stitches and 48 rows = 10 cm (4 inches)

DECREASING AND INCREASING

Decreasing   We decrease on end stitches; fully-fashioned increasing and decreasing are not suitable. In this rib *decreasing 1 stitch* means *1 stitch on*

99

both beds. It is possible simply to transfer the end main bed stitch to the next one, and the same on the rib bed, decreasing at both ends in the same row.

However, this is not the best method as it produces rather a tight edge. Try it this way.

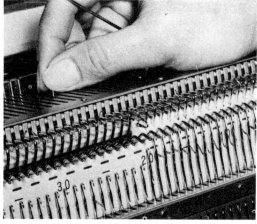

TOP LEFT: *Transfer end rib bed stitch to end main bed needle*

ABOVE: *Push needle forward so main bed stitch is behind latch, rib bed one in front. Manually knit back stitch off over front*

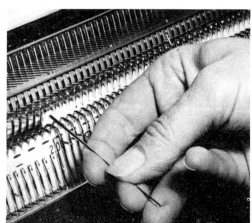

LEFT: *Transfer end main bed stitch to second main bed needle – 1 stitch has been decreased*

Cast on a practice piece. It need not be very wide, but weighting is easier if you have more than 40 stitches on the main bed. Knit 10 rows.

Decrease 1 stitch at both ends of the next row and every following 4th row 6 times in all.

You have decreased 12 stitches, NOT 24. Remember 1 from each bed only counts as 1 stitch.

Increasing This is done on the end stitches and must be done at the carriage end. It takes 2 rows to increase 1 stitch at both ends.

ABOVE: At right push 1 extra needle on both beds to holding position with the carriages set to knit the needles back. It is much quicker to push needles right out than to leave them in working position. Knit 1 row

ABOVE RIGHT: A row has been knitted. The increasing shows as a figure-of-eight round the new end needles

RIGHT: The same again at the left

VARIATION 1: LONG STITCH

Cast on as before over 60 main bed needles using waste yarn. After knitting selvedge, set carriages for pattern which is automatic, that is, the setting remains the same throughout. Tension 2/2.

Main bed: Knit in both directions
Rib bed: Slip to left, so no change

Knit 10 rows waste, 60 rows main yarn, marking 21st main bed stitches as before. Knit 10 rows waste yarn. Cast off.

Look carefully at both sides of fabric. The side facing you has longer stitches, which is how it gets its name. It can be knitted with the settings of the two beds reversed, in which case the long stitch side, which is the right side, would be away from you as you knit.

Sometimes one way is more convenient than the other, as with the collar, when we need right side facing.

Tension piece measures 34 stitches and 64 rows = 10 cm (4 inches)

VARIATION 2: PIN TUCKS OR RIDGE STITCH

Cast on as before over 60 main bed needles using waste yarn. Knit selvedge and 10 rows in waste. Tension 4/4. Change to main yarn. RC 000.

A single pin tuck or ridge is made by setting one of the beds to slip, and leaving the other knitting for a number of rows. The more rows you knit with the one bed, the larger the ridges will be. We will knit four row ridges on the rib bed. The right side will therefore face us as we knit. Any number of rows can be knitted between the ridges. The setting of the main carriage must be changed every time a ridge is knitted.

Rows 1–6   Both beds knit
Rows 7–10   Main bed: Slip in both directions
                    Rib bed: Knit in both directions, so no change

Repeat these 10 rows to RC 60 marking 21st stitches on row 34. This puts the markers on the right side in a plain section. Knit 10 rows waste yarn. Cast off.

You will notice that we are using a higher tension for this stitch. If the stitches are too small, by the time you come to the last row of the four rows on the main bed alone, you will find that they will not all knit. Some will just tuck. A great deal depends upon the yarn you are using. Sometimes it is easier to take the close knit bar out and to put an extra weight on. If the main bed needles are pushed to holding position before the fourth row they are certain to knit, but this should not really be necessary.

102

Ridge stitch or pin tucks

Tension piece measures 31 stitches and 54 rows = 10 cm (4 inches)

TO KNIT THE TEE SHIRT

This pattern is written for a garment with 2 × 2 rib welts as knitted in Chapter 7, and the main pieces in Full Needle rib. The sleeves will be knitted with narrow welts to prevent stretching of the edge, but the back and front could be loose if you wish, starting at the bottom with full needle rib. Alternative instructions are given for this below. The collar and pockets can be knitted in full needle rib as given in the pattern, or in one of the variations. The instructions for collar alternatives are also given below.

The welts are knitted in 2 by 2 ribbing, 2 up 1 down version, knitting at Tension 1./1.. (Refer to Chapter 7 if necessary.)

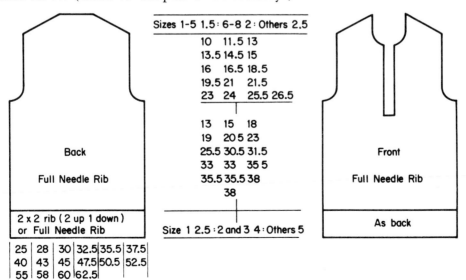

Sizes 1-5 1.5 : 6-8 2 : Others 2.5

10 11.5 13
13.5 14.5 15
16 16.5 18.5
19.5 21 21.5
23 24 25.5 26.5

13 15 18
19 20 5 23
25.5 30.5 31.5
33 33 35 5
35.5 35.5 38
38

Size 1 2.5 : 2 and 3 4 : Others 5

Back

Full Needle Rib

2 x 2 rib (2 up 1 down)
or Full Needle Rib

25	28	30	32.5	35.5	37.5
40	43	45	47.5	50.5	52.5
55	58	60	62.5		

Front

Full Needle Rib

As back

The front band is knitted in circular knitting, and, together with the collar and pocket, can be in a contrast colour, as in the original. The tension used was 4/4, and the circular tension swatch measured as follows:

36 stitches (both beds, so 72 in the round) and 112 rows = 10 cm (4 inches)

The buttonhole side of the band is knitted first, followed by a long piece of circular knitting for the button side. The work is released on circular waste knitting. After sewing to the garment, surplus length is unravelled and the edge stitches oversewn together through the loops.

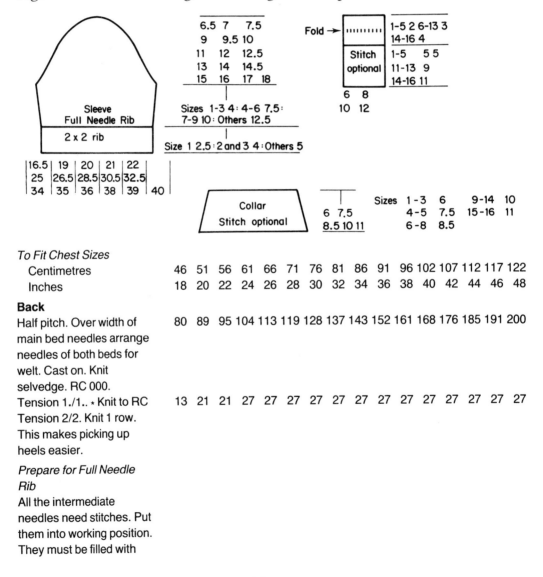

6.5 7   7.5
9   9.5 10
11   12   12.5
13   14   14.5
15   16   17 18

Sizes 1-3 4: 4-6 7.5:
7-9 10: Others 12.5

Size 1 2.5: 2 and 3 4: Others 5

Sleeve
Full Needle Rib
2 x 2 rib

16.5	19	20	21	22
25	26.5	28.5	30.5	32.5
34	35	36	38	39	40

Fold → |·········| 1-5 2 6-13 3
                     14-16 4
         Stitch   1-5   5 5
         optional   11-13 9
                     14-16 11
         6   8
         10 12

Collar
Stitch optional

6 7.5
8.5 10 11

Sizes 1-3 6   9-14 10
       4-5 7.5   15-16 11
       6-8 8.5

To Fit Chest Sizes																
Centimetres	46	51	56	61	66	71	76	81	86	91	96	102	107	112	117	122
Inches	18	20	22	24	26	28	30	32	34	36	38	40	42	44	46	48

Back

Half pitch. Over width of main bed needles arrange needles of both beds for welt. Cast on. Knit selvedge. RC 000.

80	89	95	104	113	119	128	137	143	152	161	168	176	185	191	200

Tension 1./1.. ∗ Knit to RC Tension 2/2. Knit 1 row. This makes picking up heels easier.

13	21	21	27	27	27	27	27	27	27	27	27	27	27	27	27

Prepare for Full Needle Rib

All the intermediate needles need stitches. Put them into working position. They must be filled with heels from the opposite bed. If you just knit you will pick up loops on the empty needles and make a row of holes, so that is not the method to use. With the beds in half pitch picking up heels is tricky. Put rib bed to full pitch. You have:

```
MB    | | o | | o | | o | | o | |
RB    o | | o | | o | | o | | o
```

Now it is easy to see which heel goes on which needle. When you have finished GO BACK TO HALF PITCH.
You now have Full Needle rib arrangement:

```
MB    | | | | | | | | | | | | | |
RB    | | | | | | | | | | | | | |
```

Set machine for circular knitting:
Main bed slip to left, rib bed slip to right.
Tension 2/2. Knit 2 rows. This is easier, especially in fine yarn with small tensions, than going straight into Full Needle rib *.

   NOTE : Omit * to * if you do not knit welt and cast on for Full Needle rib knitting extra rows:
Size 1 12
Sizes 2–3 20
Other Sizes 24 rows
Increase 1 Stitch on Both Beds in sizes 2 3 5 6 8 9 11 14 15.
Number of stitches given means stitches ON BOTH BEDS THROUGHOUT:
Set both carriages to knit.
RC 000. Knit to RC

80	90	96	104	114	120	128	138	144	152	162	168	176	186	192	200
60	72	84	90	96	108	120	144	150	156	156	168	168	168	180	180

REMEMBER : extra rows here if no welt knitted.

Armhole Shaping Use method already practised for all casting off and decreasing. RC 000. At beginning of next 2 rows cast off

Sizes 4–5 At beginning of next 2 rows cast off

Sizes 6–16 At beginning of next 4 rows cast off

All Sizes At both ends of next row and following alternate rows decrease 1 stitch the following number of times

Stitches remaining

Knit to RC

	1	2	3	4	5	6	7	8	9	10	11	12	13	14	15	16
Armhole cast off (next 2 rows)	4	4	5	5	5	5	5	5	5	5	5	5	6	6	6	6
Sizes 4–5 cast off				2	2											
Sizes 6–16 cast off						2	2	2	3	3	3	3	3	3	3	3
Decrease 1 st number of times	6	7	7	6	7	6	7	8	7	7	9	10	10	10	12	13
Stitches remaining	60	68	72	78	86	90	96	104	108	116	122	126	132	142	144	150
Knit to RC	48	54	60	64	70	72	76	78	88	94	100	102	108	114	120	126

Shoulder Shaping by casting off in groups as follows at beginning of next 6, 8 or 12 rows

	1	2	3	4	5	6	7	8	9	10	11	12	13	14	15	16
	6	6	7	8	6	7	7	5	5	6	6	6	7	7	7	8
	5	6	7	7	6	7	7	5	5	6	6	6	7	7	7	7
	5	6	6	7	6	6	7	5	5	6	6	6	6	7	7	7
					6	6	6	5	5	5	6	6	6	7	7	7
								5	5	5	5	6	6	7	7	7
								4	5	5	5	5	6	6	7	7
Total for each shoulder	16	18	20	22	24	26	27	29	30	33	34	35	38	41	42	43
Number of rows for shoulder shaping	6	6	6	6	8	8	8	12	12	12	12	12	12	12	12	12
Back Neck stitches. Cast off remaining	28	32	32	34	38	38	42	46	48	50	54	56	56	60	60	64

Front

Division for front opening is before armhole. Knit as back to RC

Front Opening Using length of spare yarn cast off stitches in centre as follows

	1	2	3	4	5	6	7	8	9	10	11	12	13	14	15	16
Knit as back to RC	* 54	66	78	78	84	96	104	128	134	138	138	146	146	146	158	158
Front Opening cast off centre	8	8	8	8	8	8	8	10	10	10	10	10	10	12	12	12

Set both carriages to hold. Push all stitches left of cast off to holding position. Pin wire weight hanger through front to right of cast off. Hang small weight. Continue to armhole shaping, length as back on stitches at right

36 41 44 48 53 56 60 64 67 71 76 79 83 87 90 94

Shape Armhole as back. RC 000. Knit To RC

30 36 36 40 42 44 42 48 58 58 64 66 72 72 78 84

Neck Shaping at left cast off

3 4 4 4 6 6 7 7 7 7 8 9 9 10 10 10

Knit 2 rows. Decrease 1 stitch at neck edge every row following number of times

7 8 8 9 9 9 10 11 12 13 14 14 14 14 14 16

Knit to shoulder shaping RC as back.

Shoulder Shaping as for back, start at right.

Second Side Return RC to *. Reverse all shaping.

Sleeves Knit 2 alike Half pitch. Over width of main bed needles arrange needles of both beds for welt. Cast on. Knit selvedge. RC 000.

53* 62 65* 68 71* 80 86 92 98 104 110 113* 116 122 125* 128

Tension 1./1.. Knit to RC Tension 2/2. Knit 1 row. Prepare for Full Needle rib as before. Increase 1 stitch on both beds

13 21 21 27 27 27 27 27 27 27 27 27 27 27 27 27

sizes marked * to Increase at both ends as follows:

54 62 66 68 72 80 86 92 98 104 110 114 116 122 126 128

Sizes 1–3 4th and every following 4th row 3 times in all.

Sizes 4–6 6th and every following 6th row 4 times in all.

Sizes 7–16 8th and every following 8th row following number of times

5 4 5 5 5 5 6 5 5 6

Number of stitches

60 68 72 76 80 88 96 100 108 114 120 124 128 132 136 140

Sleeve Head RC 000. At beginning of next 2 rows cast off following number of stitches   4 4 5 4 5 5 5 4 5 4 5 5 6 6 5 5

Knit 2 rows. Decrease
1 stitch at both ends of
next row and every
following alternate row
following number of times   12 14 14 18 19 21 23 26 27 28 29 31 32 34 37 39

At beginning of next   4 4 6 4 4 4 4 4 4 6 6 6 6 4 4 4

rows cast off following
number of stitches   3 4 3 2 2 3 4 4 3 3 3 2 2 2 2 2

Knit 2 rows. Cast off
remaining stitches   16 16 16 24 24 24 24 24 32 32 34 40 40 44 44 44

RC   32 36 38 44 46 50 54 60 62 66 68 72 74 76 82 86

Seam shoulders ready for
attaching collar.

**Button and Buttonhole
Placket** One piece.
Circular strip. Tension 0/0.
Cast on (both beds)   10 10 10 10 10 10 12 12 12 12 12 12 12 14 14 14

Use wire weight hanger
and small weight. Knit
2 rows at each of following
tensions Tension 1/1;
Tension 2/2; Tension 3/3.
Change to full pitch.
Tension 4/4. RC 000.
Starting with buttonhole
half knit to RC   12 all sizes

RC 000. Knit to RC   28 36 36 46 48 50 56 38 42 46 50 52 40 40 42 46

Sizes 1–8 8 row
buttonholes.
Sizes 9–16 12 row
buttonholes.

To Make Buttonhole Set
both carriages to hold.
Push needles of left half
on both beds to holding
position. Knit 8 (12) rows
on right of strip. Break off
yarn. Push right needles to
holding position. Move
carriage to left. Bring left
half to upper working
position. Knit 8 (12) rows
on left of strip. Bring right
half to upper working
position. RC 000.

Rows Between Buttonholes

| Knit to RC | 28 | 36 | 36 | 46 | 48 | 50 | 56 | 38 | 42 | 46 | 50 | 52 | 40 | 40 | 42 | 46 |

Make another buttonhole.

| *Number of Buttonholes* | 2 | 2 | 2 | 2 | 2 | 2 | 2 | 3 | 3 | 3 | 3 | 3 | 4 | 4 | 4 | 4 |

Continue until all buttonholes have been made. RC 000. After last buttonhole knit to RC

| | 96 | 112 | 112 | 132 | 136 | 140 | 152 | 162 | 186 | 198 | 210 | 216 | 232 | 240 | 240 | 246 |

Waste yarn. Knit 12 rows. Release from machine. Using a wool needle take all the ends on the buttonholes through the tube to the edge which will be sewn to the opening on the front, and fasten them off in the seam. No stitching is needed on the buttonholes themselves.

Collar Over width of Full

Needle rib	80	86	92	98	106	114	120	124	130	136	140	146	152	158	164	170
Long Stitch	85	91	98	106	115	121	128	132	138	145	149	155	161	168	174	180
Ridge Stitch	78	83	89	95	105	110	116	120	126	132	136	141	147	153	159	165

Main bed needles cast on and knit selvedge.

Collar is shaped by tension change as follows:

Full Needle Rib; Long Stitch 1/3 total rows knitted at each of: 2../2.. 2./2. 2/2.

Full Needle Rib Total rows	30	30	30	36	36	42	42	42	48	48	48	48	48	48	54	54
Rows to be knitted at each tension	10	10	10	12	12	14	14	14	16	16	16	16	16	16	18	18
Long Stitch Total rows	42	42	42	48	48	54	54	54	66	66	66	66	66	66	72	72
Rows to be knitted at each tension	14	14	14	16	16	18	18	18	22	22	22	22	22	22	24	24

Ridge Stitch Total rows
Tensions: 4../4.. 4./4. 4/4.

| Ridge Stitch | 36 | 36 | 36 | 42 | 42 | 48 | 48 | 48 | 54 | 54 | 54 | 54 | 54 | 54 | 66 | 66 |

| Rows to be knitted at each tension | 12 | 12 | 12 | 14 | 14 | 16 | 16 | 16 | 18 | 18 | 18 | 18 | 18 | 18 | 22 | 22 |

Set for circular knitting. Tension 4/4. Knit 6 rows. Transfer all stitches to

main bed. Place neckline
of garment on needles
wrong side facing.
Tension 10. Knit 1 row.
Cast off.

Pocket Only 1 shown.
Stitch to match collar.
Make more if you wish.
Arrange for Full Needle
rib. Cast on over
main bed needles. Knit
selvedge. RC 000. Knit to
Transfer for 2 × 2 rib.
RC 000. Knit to
Transfer stitches to main
bed. Release on waste
knitting.

20	20	20	20	20	26	26	26	26	26	32	32	32	38	38	38
28	28	28	28	28	34	34	34	34	34	44	44	44	54	54	54
12	12	12	12	12	16	16	16	16	16	16	16	16	20	20	20

To Make Up Sew buttonhole placket in position, backstitching fold to opening on front. Sew on buttons to match buttonholes. Sew side seams, leaving 5 to 7.5 cm (2 to 3 inch) vent if there is no rib. Sew sleeve seams. Pin and tack sleeves into armholes. Sew into position.

NOTE: Expert operators with sewing machines may wish to sew up with them. This is quite acceptable for experts. If your machining does not look professional use mattress stitching which, if properly done, does! Fold pocket rib to inside, hemming through the stitch loops. Place pocket in position. Tack and sew.

TO RECAP

In this chapter you have learnt:
how to cast on and knit Full Needle rib and two variations
three ways of casting off this stitch
increasing and decreasing
making buttonholes in a tubular edging strip by using the holding method...
and...
you have been given a tee shirt pattern in 16 sizes.

11

SHAPING AN A-LINE SKIRT KNITTED IN ENGLISH RIB BY TENSION CHANGE

The last two projects in this first ribbing course are an English rib skirt and a jacket to match, the skirt in this chapter and the jacket in Chapter 12.

From the photograph you will see that in the original two colours have been used. This is a matter of choice: one colour could have been used throughout. The stripes used were 8 rows main colour and 4 rows contrast colour. This amount of colour-changing could be done without a colour changer if you do not have one.

This A-line skirt is simple to knit, and English rib is a very suitable stitch for it, because it hangs well and does not drop in wear. Being a tuck rib it produces a comparatively wide fabric, and this means that there is room on the machine for quite large sizes to be knitted with just two panels.

For even larger sizes, three panels can be used, because, of course, your seaming is now quite invisible!

Shaping the skirt is also easy. It used to be done by decreasing on the sides from hip-line to waist. However, end stitch decreasing is very difficult to sew up neatly and unobtrusively, and it is therefore far better to use the method which is known as 'shaping by tension change'. That is the method used in this pattern.

For the skirt and jacket 4 ply wool or wool mix is recommended. The tension used was 4/4, and the measurements of the tension swatch after washing, drying and blocking out were:

28 stitches and 56 rows = 10 cm (4 inches)

Those knitters who use Jones + Brother machines can knit English rib with the Slide Lever on II. When this is done the tension on both beds needs to be higher by approximately two whole numbers. The resulting knitting is firmer and very suitable for skirts and jackets.

All machine knitters know that a sample knitted at a higher tension will be larger, and one knitted at a lower tension will be smaller. We are going to use five different tensions in the skirt, but we are not going to knit five different tension swatches. First, we knit just the one, using tension 4/4. If you are using the same colour for both garments, the measurements should be the same. In different colours they may be slightly different, since the intensity of dye can have an effect. Both yarns used in the garments in the photograph on Page 4 gave measurements as above.

Now try an experiment. Cast on another piece 61 stitches wide and knit the selvedge. Then knit 12 rows at each of the following tensions: 4../4.. 4./4. 4/4 3../3.. 3./3. – a total of 60 rows. Release on waste knitting, rest and then measure the piece.

You will find that the second piece is exactly the same length as the first. The width at the top is narrower, and at the bottom wider, than the original tension swatch. These are the two facts on which we base the shaping of the skirt.

Each panel consists of two straight pieces, with a fifth of the total number of rows knitted at each of the given tensions. Just as in the test piece, the length will be the same as if the whole panel had been knitted at tension 4/4, the main tension. This is because the greater length of the larger tension sections has been balanced exactly by the shorter length of the rows knitted at the smaller tensions.

The section knitted at the main tension comes below the hip line, but its measurement is used to calculate the number of stitches for each panel.

The steps necessary for calculating the pattern for this type of skirt are as follows:

1. Take hip, waist and length measurements of person.
2. Make tension swatch at main tension – in this case 4/4.
3. Calculate total rows and divide by 5. WRITE DOWN ROW NUMBERS for each tension. These figures are given in Skirt 1 (see below).
4. Add 5 cm (2 inches) to hip measurement for ease of movement. Calculate number of stitches required.

It is important that the skirt should not be bulky round the waist, and the section at the smallest tension may not make it quite small enough. To

112

overcome this the last section can be divided into two halves. The first half is knitted at tension 3./3. and the second at tension 3/3. Great care is then taken, as will be explained in the pattern, to make a waistband which is not thick and clumsy. If this suggestion is adopted it will be necessary to add 6 rows to the first section to make the length correct. The figures given for Skirt 2 (see below) are calculated on this basis.

TO KNIT THE SKIRT

To Fit Waist Sizes	Centimetres				61	66	71	76	81	86	91	96	102
	Inches				24	26	28	30	32	34	36	38	40
Hip Sizes	Centimetres				86	91	96	102	107	112	117	122	127
	Inches				34	36	38	40	42	44	46	48	50
Skirt measurements at hip in centimetres					91	96	102	107	112	117	122	131	137

Skirt 1

Tension				4../4..	4./4.	4/4	3../3..	3./3.
Length								
A	66 cm (26 inches)	370 rows	Knit to RC	74	148	222	296	370
B	71 cm (28 inches)	400 rows		80	160	240	320	400
C	76 cm (30 inches)	430 rows		86	172	258	344	430

Skirt 2

Tension				4../4..	4./4.	4/4	3../3..	3./3.	3/3
Length									
A	66 cm (26 inches)	376 rows	Knit to RC	80	154	228	302	340	376
B	71 cm (28 inches)	406 rows		86	166	246	326	366	406
C	76 cm (30 inches)	436 rows		92	178	264	350	394	436

Knit 2 panels alike.

Waist Size	61	66	71	76	81	86	91	96	102
	127	135	143	149	157	163	171	177	185

Arrange needles for English rib as follows
Cast on and knit selvedge. Change to English rib setting. RC 000. Knit panel changing tension as given for chosen length, either Skirt 1 or Skirt 2.

Waistband Transfer all stitches to main bed. Tension 6. Knit 1 row. Transfer all rib bed stitches to adjacent needles pushing empty needles to non-working position.

MB | o | o | o | o | o |

Tension 4. Knit 12 rows. Bring empty needles to working position. Tension 10. Knit 1 row. Cast off with latch tool working from needle to needle and treating loops cast on in last row as if they were stitches. This makes a cast off edge which is not too tight for the waist line.

TO LINE AND MAKE UP THE SKIRT

All knitted skirts are better lined. This prevents clinging and seating, and skirts hang and move better. Before sewing up cut the two lining pieces using the knitting as a guide. Cut the lining 5 cm (2 inches) wider than the knitting at both sides. This is quite a lot wider, but it includes the seams, and it should also be remembered that the knitting will stretch and the lining will not. The top of the lining will be turned in and sewn to the bottom of the waistband, so allow for that turning in the length. The lining should be 2.5 to 3 cm (1–1½ inches) shorter than the knitting after turning up the hem.

Seam the lining and press the seams. Turn over the top to the wrong side and tack. Do not turn up the hem at this stage.

Mattress stitch seams of skirt panels keeping rib formation exactly right. Sew waistband to the inside leaving 1 cm (½ inch) open for threading elastic. The best stitch to use is herring-bone stitch because it stretches.

Pin lining to the bottom of the waistband stretching the knitting to fit. Sew lining into position. Sew two tape loops inside for hanging. Thread in the elastic. Leave the skirt hanging for a day or two before hemming up the lining.

TO RECAP

In this chapter you have learnt:

a simple method of shaping an A-line skirt applicable to any rib which is not too elastic

how to knit a neat waistband

how to line a skirt . . . and . . .

you have been given a skirt pattern in English rib in nine sizes

12

SADDLE-SHOULDER JACKET KNITTED IN ENGLISH RIB WITH COLLAR AND POCKETS IN RACKED ENGLISH RIB

The last project in this ribbing course is a jacket to complement the skirt knitted in Chapter 11. If the same colour is used you will not need a tension swatch for the main pieces of the garment. The measurements will be the same as for the skirt, knitting at tension 4/4. Only the collar will be different. That will be knitted in RACKED English rib and will need a separate tension swatch. (See Pages 4, 7 and 8.)

If stripes are knitted, pull down a loop of contrast yarn between stripes when knitting the right front and the collar to avoid floats on the edge of the knitting. The loops can then be cut through and the ends threaded across the back and fastened off. Stripes can be any depth the knitter chooses. In the original they are 8 rows main colour, 4 rows contrast colour. The trims are more effective knitted in the contrast colour if one is used.

So far we have only used the racking facility to enable us to cast on the 2 by 2 ribs. However there are some very attractive stitch patterns in which racking is used throughout. Some of these are given in the ribber instruction books, and it would be a good idea to try them out.

Don't be afraid to have a go at new ideas! Now you have knitted nearly all the projects in this course you are a much more experienced knitter than you were at the beginning. Just read the instructions carefully – AND TAKE IT ONE STEP AT A TIME!

The principle on which all racked stitches are based is a very simple one. The rib bed is moved either to right or to left, often by only one needle place, sometimes more. This, provided you have set up your machine correctly, places the stitches in a different order of knitting from that of the previous row. We can easily understand this if we sit at the machine and pretend to knit the pattern before actually getting involved with yarn. That is what we will do before knitting a tension swatch for the collar.

Arrange some needles for 1 by 1 rib – full pitch position, racking handle on 5. Place the carriage at the right.

```
MB     | o | o | o | o |
RB       o | o | o | o |
```

Stitches cast on ready for English rib. Beds in full pitch position

Now turn the racking handle so that the rib bed moves one place to the right. The number you rack to is 4 if you are using a Jones + Brother or Knitmaster machine, 6 if you are using a Toyota. What you now have is this:

```
MB     | o | o | o | o |
RB       o | o | o | o |
```

Rib bed racked 1 place to right when in full pitch position

Obviously that will not do! If you knit that row you will be very sorry! AND SO WILL YOUR MACHINE!

You could rack to the right again. That would give you this arrangement:

```
MB     | o | o | o | o |
RB     o o o | o | o | o |
```

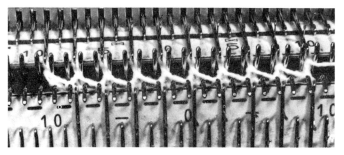

Rib bed racked 2 places to right when in full pitch position

116

That has changed the order in which the stitches will knit, but you needed two turns of the racking handle to get there, and you will need two turns to get back to the start . . . There is a much easier way. Start again with the first needle arrangement, but this time set the rib bed to half pitch. This is what happens:

MB | o | o | o | o |
RB   o | o | o | o |

Stitches cast on ready for English rib. Beds in half pitch position. Note that they are in the same order as at the beginning

With just one turn of the racking handle we move the rib bed stitches over into their second position:

MB | o | o | o | o |
RB   o | o | o | o |

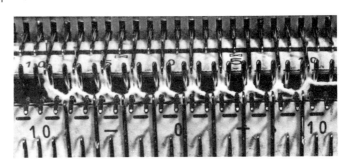

Rib bed racked 1 place to right with beds in half position. Note how racking 1 place is sufficient when beds are in this position

If you rack back to the left then once again the needles will be arranged as they were in the beginning.

Racked English rib is made by knitting 2 rows with the needles in the first position and 2 rows with them in the second position.

Now, if you wish, you can follow the instructions in your own ribber manual, because the various manuals differ somewhat about the order in which you knit the 4-row sequence. It makes no difference to the fabric, as long as you keep to the same sequence throughout. We are going to knit a tension swatch, so you should knit it either by the method given in your manual, or the way I do it, which is given below. The racking must follow the tuck rows.

TO KNIT A TENSION SWATCH IN RACKED ENGLISH RIB
Full pitch, both carriages to knit. Racking handle on 5. Arrange 61 needles for 1 by 1 rib. Cast on and knit selvedge. Carriage right. RC 000. Set the machine for racked English rib as follows:

> Tension 4./4.
>
> Half pitch
>
> Either Main bed to tuck to the left and rib bed to knit both ways
>
> or Rib bed to tuck to the left and main bed to knit both ways

Can you remember which side will be the right side if you tuck on the main bed? It is the same as the unracked version, of course.

Knit 1 row. Carriage left. * Rack 1 place to right (Knitmaster and Jones + Brother 4, Toyota 6). Knit 2 rows. Carriage left. Rack 1 place to left (All machines 5). Knit 2 rows *. Repeat from * to * to RC 60 marking the 21st stitches both sides of centre on the 30th row in the usual way.

You will find that row 60 is a row knitted to the right after you have racked back to 5.

If you knit this particular row sequence all the racking is done when the carriage is at the left, and as the racking handle is also at the left you may think, as I do, that there is some advantage in not trying to look at both ends of the machine at once!

Let it become automatic, but, even so, be careful not to rack in the wrong direction.

If you are interrupted in the middle, keep the interruption at bay until you have knitted to the end where you know you are not going to rack. There is an indicator to tell you whether you have racked or not . . . (Have you? . . . Haven't you? . . . Yes . . . No . . . I don't know!) Just let the 'phone bell ring until the carriage is at the non-racking end!

Change to waste yarn. Knit 12 rows and release the work from the machine. Rest the fabric and measure. The measurements of the swatch used for the collar were:

> 28 stitches and 60 rows = 10 cm (4 inches)

You will notice that we needed a slightly higher tension to give the same width measurement as the unracked English rib. (Jones + Brother machines: Slide Lever 1. Tension as other machines.)

TO KNIT THE JACKET
The jacket is knitted with saddle shoulders, and the pattern is given in sizes to

go with the skirt pattern. In standard British measurements it is assumed that the hip measurement is 5 cm (2 inches) greater than the bust measurement. It is, of course, necessary to measure the person for whom the garment is intended, and make adjustments as required.

Perhaps this will be for you!

The front bands are knitted as extra stitches on each front. English rib has a very neat edging, and, since there are no welts in a different rib, it is appropriate to incorporate the bands without a join. If buttons are required a suitable method is to mark buttonhole positions with short lengths of waste yarn and crochet round the loops afterwards. It is possible to strengthen the buttonholes, which will probably be 5 stitches wide, by crocheting over a cord.

You will not want tuck stitches in the marked buttonhole position. Prevent them by knitting the marker threads in manually after a row in which both beds have knitted. Leave the buttonhole needles in upper working position for the next row, and then they will knit back, resuming the English rib formation in the following rows.

The underside of the button front should be strengthened with tape, and a smaller button should be sewn behind each face button to prevent pulling. Both buttons are sewn on together.

I have purposely not suggested exact size and position for buttons for this jacket. This is YOUR choice. Do try knitting and finishing a practice buttonhole before you incorporate them in the right front. It is a good idea to knit the left front first, and then check out how many buttons you need, and where they should be placed. When counting rows remember 1 fat loop = 2 rows.

For all but the first two or three sizes in this pattern a bust dart should be incorporated in both fronts unless the jacket fits loosely. These can be knitted in by the use of short row knitting, as given in the basic instructions for the single bed machine. The disadvantage of this method is that if the dart is not in exactly the right position, it will not fit well, and it cannot be altered without a lot of unpicking.

Another method is to knit extra length on each front, and fit the dart accurately on the person (garment inside out) as you would in dressmaking. From 10 to 14 rows extra would be needed, according to size. After pinning and tacking use a sewing machine to sew the dart.

119

TO ADAPT THE PATTERN TO A PULLOVER

This pattern can very easily be adapted for use as a round-necked pullover by casting on the same number of stitches for the front as for the back, thus omitting the extra stitches allowed on the jacket fronts for the bands. The garment would need to be about 5 cm (2 inches) shorter and to include a 1 by 1 ribbed welt in the remaining length. The tension for the welts would be 3/3.

When dividing for the neck, transfer stitches on the left to the main bed and set it to hold. If a lady's pullover is knitted it can have a collar as given for the jacket, or it can have a 1 by 1 rib neckband. Use the same number of stitches for the band as for the collar. Remember to knit a third of the band at 2./2., a third at 2../2.. and a third at 3/3.

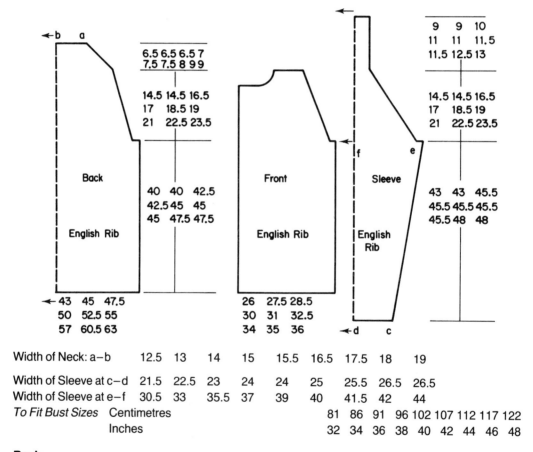

Width of Neck: a–b		12.5	13	14	15	15.5	16.5	17.5	18	19	

Width of Sleeve at c–d	21.5	22.5	23	24	24	25	25.5	26.5	26.5	
Width of Sleeve at e–f	30.5	33	35.5	37	39	40	41.5	42	44	

To Fit Bust Sizes	Centimetres		81	86	91	96	102	107	112	117	122
	Inches		32	34	36	38	40	42	44	46	48

Back

Arrange needles for English rib as follows   121 127 135 141 149 155 163 169 177
Cast on. Knit selvedge. Tension zig zag row 0/0; circular
row 1/1. RC 000. Set rib bed to tuck to left, main bed to
knit both ways. Wrong side of fabric facing. Knit to RC   224 224 238 238 252 252 252 266 266

120

* *Armhole and Saddle Shaping* RC 000. At beginning of next 2 rows cast off

6	7	7	7	7	7	9	9	9

There are now 2 sloping sections. The 1st is gradual, the 2nd is much quicker.

1st Slope Decrease 1 stitch at both ends on every following

6	7	7	7	7	7	8	8	8

rows until following stitches have been decreased at both sides

13	4	7	8	4	4	2	10	16

Decrease 1 stitch at both ends on every following rows until following extra stitches have been decreased at both sides

–	6	6	6	6	6	7	7	–
–	9	7	7	12	13	14	6	–

Total cast off and decreased at both sides

19	20	21	22	23	24	25	25	25

Stitches remaining

83	87	93	97	103	107	113	119	127

** RC

80	84	94	100	102	108	116	124	128

Turn back to RC 000.

2nd Slope Decreasing now takes place more frequently as follows:
Sizes 1 2 9 Decrease 1 stitch both ends; knit 1 row; then decrease 1 stitch both ends and knit 2 rows. That is 2 stitches both ends every 3 rows. Repeat these 3 rows until following number of extra stitches have been decreased at both sides

24	25	–	–	–	–	–	–	36

Other Sizes Decrease 1 stitch both ends; knit 2 rows; then [decrease 1 stitch both ends; knit 1 row] twice. That is 3 stitches both ends every 4 rows. Repeat these 4 rows until following number of extra stitches have been decreased at both sides

–	–	27	28	29	30	32	34	–

Stitches remaining

35	37	39	41	45	47	49	51	55

Knit following extra rows

0	1	2	0	2	2	0	1	2

RC

36	38	38	40	42	42	44	52	54

Cast off remaining stitches loosely for back neck.

Left Front
Arrange needles for English rib as follows:
half back (approx.)

61	65	69	71	75	79	83	85	89

and for band

12	All sizes	

total

73	77	81	83	87	91	95	97	101

Knit as back to armhole and saddle shaping on left edge. RC 000. Knit as back from * to ** decreasing on left, keeping right straight to RC

68	70	80	86	86	92	100	108	112

Continue armhole shaping. AT SAME TIME at beginning of next row at neck edge (right) cast off

25	26	27	27	28	30	31	31	33

Knit 1 row. Decrease 1 stitch at neck edge on next and every following alternate row following number of times

5	6	6	6	7	7	7	7	7

Stitches remaining

24	25	27	28	29	30	32	34	36

Knit 1 or 2 extra rows if required to RC

80	84	94	100	102	108	116	124	128

Cast off.

Sleeves Knit 2 alike.

Arrange needles for English rib as follows	61	63	65	67	69	71	73	75	77
Knit to RC	36	38	38	40	42	42	44	52	54
rows, the following number of times in all	14	16	19	20	20	21	22	23	24
Number of stitches	89	95	103	107	109	113	117	121	125
Knit without shaping to RC	240	240	254	254	254	254	254	268	268

Sleeve Head and Saddle Shaping RC 000.

At beginning of next 2 rows cast off	6	7	7	7	7	7	9	9	9

Sizes 7–9 Knit 3 rows. Decrease 1 stitch both ends of next row and every following 4th row following number of times

							12	17	18

All Sizes Knit 2 rows. Decrease 1 stitch both ends of next and every following 3rd row the following number of times

	24	26	30	31	32	35	22	18	18

Sizes 1–5 Knit 1 row. Decrease 1 stitch both ends of next row and every following alternate row following number of times

	3	2	1	2	2				
Knit to RC	80	84	94	100	102	108	116	124	128
Stitches remaining	23	25	27	27	27	29	31	33	35
RC 000. Knit without shaping to RC	50	50	56	62	62	64	64	70	72

Cast off loosely.

Collar

Arrange needles for English rib as follows

	117	125	133	137	145	153	161	168	181

Cast on and knit selvedge in full pitch position. RC 000. Change to half pitch position and knit in racked English rib. Knit the following number of rows at each of these tensions, thus shaping collar by tension change: 5/5 4../4.. 4./4.

	16	16	16	18	18	18	18	20	20
Total rows	48	48	48	54	54	54	54	60	60

Rack to 5 (if not already on 5). Change to full pitch and 1 × 1 rib. Knit 6 rows. Cast off in rib.

Pockets Knit 2 alike.

Knit in English rib. Tension 4./4..

Stitches	35	35	35	37	37	37	37	39	39
Rows	72	72	72	76	76	76	76	80	80

Change to 1 × 1 rib as on collar. Knit 12 rows. Cast off in rib.

   NOTE : The 1 × 1 rib at the end of collar and pockets turns to the wrong side and makes an elastic edge. Hem down on inside of pockets.

Trim for armhole and saddle seams. Knitted on main bed only (in contrast yarn if used). Make single row punchcard:

. . . . ● ● . ● ● ● . ● ● . . . .

Electronic machines: mark row of 9 squares on mylar sheet (* to *). Cast on 9 stitches to correspond with

122

punched group if using punchcard machine. Carriage right
for start of pattern.
Row 1: Right to left: Knit.
Row 2: Left to right: Slip.
  Tension 6. Knit length of trim sufficient for both
  armhole and saddle seams. Cast off.

To Make Up Use mattress stitching for all seams. Sew side and sleeve seams.
Sew saddles and sleeve heads to front and back pieces. Place trims, which fold
naturally at slip stitches, in position on right side on top of armhole and saddle
seams. Slip stitch to garment underneath each edge. Cut off surplus and finish
off ends. Sew collar to neckline, leaving 6 stitches on both fronts not attached
to collar. Hem 1 by 1 rib to inside of pockets, then mattress stitch them
into position at the bottom of each front, matching up stripes if these have
been knitted. Sew strengthening tape under left front before sewing on
buttons, or back the buttons with small buttons on the wrong side. Crochet
round buttonholes.

It proved impossible to obtain either buttons which matched the yarn used
for the stripes, or strengthening tape which matched the main jacket colour.
Crochet was therefore used as follows:

To strengthen button and buttonhole edges and prevent stretching, working
on the wrong side, crochet 6 rows of single crochet along the 6 rows of knit
stitches nearest to the edge using a 2¼ mm crochet hook. This method proved
to be very satisfactory, despite all the ends which needed to be sewn in.

To cover a button, select shank buttons a little smaller than would be
required if used uncovered. Using same size hook, make 4 chain, join into
circle. Work in a spiral (ie. not joining into rounds) as follows:

* Work 2 double crochet into 1st chain, 1 double crochet into 2nd chain *
Repeat * to * until crochet just shows when button is laid on it.
** Work 1 double crochet into each of next 2 chains, miss 1 chain **
Repeat ** to ** until enough has been worked to allow the button to be
put into position. Continue until the diameter of the space left is about
half the diameter of the button.
*** Work 1 single crochet into next chain, miss 1 chain ***
Work *** to *** until button is completely covered. Fasten off yarn. Sew
into position using backing buttons, and sewing both on at the same
time.

Optional Belt

This is very much a matter of taste, and needs trying out to suit individual requirements. Try 11, 13 or 15 stitches in racked English rib knitting at Tension 4/4. Put marker in one edge at 200 rows. When you think you have reached the end, release on waste knitting without breaking off main yarn, then you can put it back and knit some more if necessary. Back belt with stiffening and add buckle to match buttons if desired.

TO RECAP

In this chapter you have learnt:
   a little about racked ribs
   one method of allowing for bust darts
   a way of making quite large buttonholes
   how to stop buttons pulling knitwear out of shape
   how a saddle shoulder garment is knitted...and...
YOU HAVE COMPLETED YOUR FIRST RIBBER COURSE!!!

Don't go away! In the next chapter we will review our course.

13

LOOKING BACK

Here we are, then, at the end of the course. I hope you have enjoyed it, and profited by working steadily through the whole of it. Now we have come to exhibition time. All that lovely knitting, carefully and painstakingly finished, and laid out in course order ready for inspection.

Sadly, I shall not be able to inspect it for you, so I must leave you to look over it, as far as you possibly can, through my eyes. One of the things I continue to stress is achieving a professional standard. Whenever I think of professionalism I think of the difference between professional and amateur as defined by a very dear and respected friend in the world of music:

An amateur is one who practises till he gets it right. A professional is one who practises until he cannot get it wrong.

Relating that to knitting, and sewing up, we might say:

If it does not look right – UNPICK IT AND TRY AGAIN!

Inspect your work, then, with that in mind, and if there should be anything that you think does not come up to standard, perhaps you would like to practise it again...and yet again...until it is absolutely right.

Looking at all your course work, particularly if you were an absolute beginner when you started, you should feel a glow of satisfaction when you see the amount that you have learnt in this short time. If any of you wondered if you had done the right thing spending a considerable amount of money on a ribber, I hope that you now know that it was more than worth it. Encouraging, looking back, isn't it?

But...this is not the end. It is only the beginning. There is so much more we can do.

FURTHER READING

Crochet Stitches, J. & P. Coat (UK) Ltd. Glasgow, 1970

Coulston, Patricia, *Knitting Machine Maintenance*, Metropolitan Sewing Machines, Bournemouth, 1982

Twilley's Book of Instant Crochet, H. G. Twilley Ltd., 1969

Weaver, Mary, *The Ribbing Attachment Part 1*, Weaverknit Publications Ltd., 1974

    The Ribbing Attachment Part 2, Weaverknit Publications Ltd., 1976

PICTURE CREDITS

All the photographs were taken specially for the book by Kitchenham Limited of Bournemouth. The line illustrations were prepared by Chartwell Illustrators from the author's computer-generated references.

INDEX